Table Of Contents

DEDICATION

The words and spirit of this book have been created through the grace and wonder of the many people who have blessed my life. Many of their stories are recorded here and are inspiration for all of us. To all of them, and especially to my parents, Marguerite and Harry, do I dedicate this book. I am most grateful for their love. Such bread is my sabbath!

AN EXPLANATION:
The Language And Structure
Of Sabbath Bread

Awareness of the spirit, alive and active in and through our ordinary daily life, is a gift. And, as with all gifts, it must be received and responded to in order for its worth to be fully appreciated. *Sabbath Bread* offers you a way to wake up to the sacred spirit's life as the leaven of your life. It offers you some ways to receive and to respond to the gift. This book also facilitates ways for you to share the nourishment of your inner work with others, the kin of the earth. It is my hope that with *Sabbath Bread* you can come to know that your life is a revelation of the Kin-dom.

This book is named *Sabbath Bread* out of the experiences of the many peoples and individuals who have gathered with me to share our desire to know more fully the mystery of life. We have named our hunger for time, space, rituals, symbols, words, and nourishment as we searched and shared the sacred and faith realities of our lives. *Sabbath* has come to mean an interruption of the routines of our daily living. These interruptions break the repetitiveness of our less-than-conscious ways of relating with ourselves, others, and the sacred. In these "break" times or spaces, we can break through to deeper levels of relationship with ourselves, the kin of the earth, and the Kin-dom. "Sabbathing" has become a choice we make so that we can re-flect on the questions that life issues when we claim our sacred experiences.

We have also come to know that "sabbathing" is a very individual choice and pattern. One needs to know one's rhythm of life to choose where and when and how

vii

long one will sabbath. For some the need arises each day; for others it is a weekly practice. Once the nourishment of sabbath space or time is experienced, the desire for it is deepened. We have also seen the effect in our lives when we are not faithful to the sabbath. Our dependency on and/or compulsions for "fast fixes" increases in relationship to our lack of sabbath. The emptiness within increases and the quality of our relationships decreases when we omit sabbathing experiences.

Bread is a word often used to connote food or nourishment of any kind. In many instances the making of loaves of bread requires some form of leaven. *Sabbath Bread* is food for spiritual nourishment. It is leavened with the experiences of kin who seek to nurture their relationships with the values of the Kin-dom of God. One of those values is expressed in the Christian scriptures of Luke where he says that the Kin-dom of God is like a woman who put leaven into three measures of flour. (Lk. 13:20-21).

One source of knowledge tells us that a measure of flour in first century Mediterranean lands was equivalent to 25 pounds in this century's measurements. It is obvious that no one woman would have had 75 pounds of flour in the simile that Luke uses for the Kin-dom. If we are to be this good news, this gospel alive today, there are some questions we need to re-flect upon. How many peoples, that is kin, need to contribute their portion of flour for there to be three measures? Are we all asked to be the "woman" who adds the leaven? Do we remember that the Old English etymology of the word "lady" is one who kneads the loaf? And that the etymology of "lord" is the keeper of the loaf? What image of the Kin-dom rises within us when we ponder these facets? What do we need in order to harmonize the flour and leaven? Perhaps salt water. The gospel tells us that we *are* the salt of the earth! How long would the kneading take? Perhaps a sabbath!

Sabbath Bread offers you a way to discover just how much flour you have and how you are the leaven. It

viii

is one way for you to become aware of the nourishment of the Kin-dom and its kin, with whom you are called to be at home. Jesus, the revealer of the Kin-dom, issued and continues to issue the covenant call, the homing dream, through the spirit. His call was issued for all. During the last 2000 years, Christians have gathered in numerous expressions to companion each other, to share bread as kin in his name. And, as he promised, whenever and wherever we have gathered, Christ's spirit has been among us. We have broken the bread of our lives together. We have praised and thanked the sacred source of our lives for Christ's presence. We have been a eucharistic people, a bread kin, Christian companions. *Sabbath Bread* will help you to remember this reality. It will encourage you to continue to gather as bread communities for nurturing in the Kin-dom.

Sabbath Bread is a many-faceted exploration of the Christian mysteries of life. It is arranged as if it were webbings for revelation. Its contents are presented so that you can experience it as a guide for spiritual direction. The core of the book is the Re-flections. These look at the mysteries of the Kin-dom of God as it webs or weaves itself with and through our lives. It is my experience that the Kin-dom is revealed in multi-faceted ways. We come to question and mirror the revelation through our originally created gifts. Thus a book that would companion us in all our diversities and originalities must be a multi-faceted expression in itself. Therefore, the Re-flections are written in differing styles and lengths. There are stories, teachings, theological reflections, scripture rememberings, personal experiences, poetry, and prayer.

Embracing this Re-flection process of *Sabbath Bread* will at first seem messy and unsure. You may be tempted to say that it is a new language that is not worth the effort to learn to speak. Part of the reason for this experience is that the book does indeed use a language that is poetic and perhaps "foreign" to many of us. We who have been dependent on organized systems of religions for our spiritual formation are used to a standard, crafted language. The meanings of this crafted language have been interpreted by the authority. Thus, when we encounter the lure of a new imagination or the power of symbolism and poetry, and are invited to interpret it in relation to our own inner authority and personal experiences, we feel unsure, unclear, and even powerless.

Another reason that your initial experience with this book may loom as a mess is that the processes and/or exercises that are presented are of a cyclical and unmeasurable dynamic. We are more used to ladder structures and status- or achievement-measured projects. Nevertheless, I encourage you to embrace the newness, the unfamiliar, the "messes" of these processes and work with the language for some significant time before dismissing *Sabbath Bread* as "not for me."

My experience in working with many women and men who have used *Sabbath Bread* is that once they took the time and space to actually work with the processes, they began to know an inner life energy that invited them to continue such spiritual work. The language either became their own tongue, or it lured them into the formation of their own language, their own symbol system. With this language they were able to articulate their experiences of the sacred with renewing imagination. The messiness of the first encounters grew to be a freedom named "home" or "trueself."

Throughout the core of the book, the Re-flections, the Spanish word *mira* is used in order to invite you to look more deeply. *Mira* translates: *look*. I use it because it is poetically related to words such as "mirror" and "miracle." Mirrors are literal experiences of re-flections. Miracles enchant us to look with new eyes, with the seeing power of Kin-dom possibilities. *Mira* symbolically lures us to look back over, to look again at, or to re-flect with a facet of our lives, our kin's lives and the ways of the Kin-dom of God. For these same reasons the word "reflect" will be printed as "re-flect." It is in the process of "looking," of "re-flecting," or *mira* that we come to truly see the sacred presence of life webbing with our human experiences. It is in the process of seeing the differences that we come to know the harmony of oneness.

Each of the Re-flections is followed by a list of questions or insights that call you to question the mystery that the Re-flection focuses on. To be able to ask questions of the mystery of life is a power, a grace given to human creation. For too long we have been memorizing the answers to someone else's experiences of the mystery. And when our experiences don't match or resemble the answers we have memorized, we blame ourselves and mistrust our experiences. One of the spiritual disciplines that needs to be vigorously embraced in these times is the discipline of learning to ask our own questions. We need to take sabbath space and time to name our personal experiences of the holy, to re-flect on them, and to question the image of the sacred that they reveal. We need to share our questions with other kin so that, with new eyes, with Kin-dom eyes, we can praise the God who is daily incarnated in our experiences. It is my hope that Sabbath Bread will empower you to such re-flection and such questioning.

There are no "fast food" breaks within the Kin-dom of God. But Sabbath Bread will encourage you to spend time preparing feasts. If, as groups, as well as as individuals, you will covenant your presence, your time, your labor, your words, your questions, your waiting, and your silences, along with your desires for spiritual, relational, physical, mental, intuitive, and all connecting growth and wholeness, you can become companions of the Kin-dom, churches of the spirit. Freedom, at oneness, and harmony will grow among us kin. You will know yourselves as you were first known: virgin goodness. It is so natural to break bread this way.

The Re-flections section of Sabbath Bread is preceded by a portion of the book called The Mirrors. This section contains ways for you to look, mira, at your spiritual life through your religious experiences. One of the ways is through the process of "journaling." Each person has her or his own style of remembering and recording life experiences. These Mirrors help you to look at your preferred style and then to use it as you participate in the Re-flections.

The other processes that the Mirrors offer are some exercises that will aid you in personally espousing the mysteries expressed in the Re-flections. Some of these exercises are generic enough that each one of them can be used with all of the Re-flections. Other processes are specifically related to the individual Re-flection. There are a number of styles of exercises so that your own preferred gifts can be used. At times you might like to try another way so as to stretch your gifts.

The inner core of *Sabbath Bread* is followed by a manual called Sample Community Sabbaths. The manual shares some ways for seeking a faith-sharing group. It then offers designs for three differently timed possibilities of group spiritual direction, experiences, or retreats. One of these possibilities is Community Sabbath 1, Sabbath Space In Eleven Sessions, a 2 to 2½-hours per session process. The second is a week-long or seven-session process for using the Re-flections and Mirrors sections of the book. Another is a weekend-long process.

All of this manual is designed to empower you, once you have experienced the Re-flections through the Mirrors, to facilitate base communities in their desire to *mira* the Kin-dom of God. It is my hope that *Sabbath Bread* will be a helpful guide for the formation of sabbath communities who want to continue their formation in Christ beyond the many renewal programs of the churches.

This book is my thanksgiving bread to all the sacred- searching kin of my life. It is my *gracias* in word and ritual. As we continue to gather in the midst of the God of graciousness, compassion and harmony, I bless you. I hope that through *Sabbath Bread* we will continue to know the wisdom and power of the Kin- dom. I bless you and thank you with the faith and memory that:

In every generation
Wisdom chooses holy ones.
She makes them friends of God and prophets.
You are the holy one.
Live your life with abundant zest!
(Wisdom 7:27)

Be *Sabbath Bread* of the Kin-dom of God.

I.
THE
MIRRORS

HOW TO USE THE
TOOLS OF RE-FLECTION

Sabbath Bread is an invitation to the process of wisdom webbings within your ordinary daily life. Each Reflection will challenge you to grow in awareness of the spirit's movements within your journey. Christians proclaim one spirit of the triune deity. This one spirit is the source of all our energies. The spirit is the funder of our physical, mental, intuitive, sexual, and imaginative energy. All is spiritual. All is grace, a gift of the spirit. All is one. Therefore, throughout this book I will refer to the spirit's breathing in your life as your spirituality. Your spirituality is your personal, individual way of responding to the spirit's invitation to know, love, and serve the Sacred/Creating/Relating mystery of all.

How can you respond to this invitation? These Mirrors will explore some of the ways that you can respond. The inner core of Sabbath Bread offers you some possibilities and explorations of "why" a spiritually alert consciousness is necessary for Christians who are naming themselves as evangelists of the message and mission of Jesus the Christ. Sabbath Bread also describes some of the "what," some facets of our faith. These facets and connections create the webbings of spiritual consciousness or awareness. The "how" is described through the many stories of other sacred-searchers and through the processes explored in this section of the book.

When I envision the spiritual life, the sacred-searching, ever-breathing dialogue of the spirit with my life and desires, I illustrate it as a "wisdom webbing." This image parallels my experiences and re-flections more so than does the image of a journey, a castle, a direction, or a ladder. My image is not that of a spider's web but of a cobweb. Let me share some of my reflections on the cobweb and its likeness to spirituality.

A cobweb is the connection of small, almost unnoticeable particles of the atmosphere. These particles are everywhere. Yet it takes time, in a very nonlinear imagination, along with a combination of stillness, warmth, darkness, movement, chill, and light, all in an ever-evolving, ever-bonding dialogue, for the epiphany of a cobweb.

The cobweb reveals a presence of past sabbaths. The webbing is a communion of allurements, touchings, detachments, connections, and spaces. A cobweb is both an appearance of life and death. And, as a matter of experience, I seem to have to be in a sabbath space of consciousness in order to even notice its existence.

A cobweb has an unique invitational dynamic. It, rather they, draw us into themselves. "A" cobweb is a misnomer. "Cobwebbings" is closer to the reality. But, however we name its reality, we do tend to respond to them when we become aware of them. Sometimes we sit with them, watching and wondering. Sometimes we wander about releasing them with our intentions and panic. What will others think if they find cobwebbings in my environment? We know them as messy realities. At other times they lure us into meditation, a trance of thoughts that in their midst reveal past and present power. During these times we may feel almost embraced by the webbings, as if we were in a womb.

Spiritual consciousness or sabbath awareness, along with kneaded dough, baked bread, and wombs, resemble cobwebbings. It is a reality of differently shaped facets created because of a life force, the spirit, which touches and connects differently abled gifts and differently empowered tensions. What is re-flected to us is the webbings of the spirit's wisdom.

To know the wisdom of how the webbings came to be demands time, space, work, death to our illusions

and expectations, and communion with others who are
alert to the breathing of the spirit. We need to stay
awake and watch life. *Mira!* Wisdom webbings lure our
response. They draw us into a womb of challenge and
evolution. In this womb we experience communion because the essence of the womb is a communion. Wisdom
webbings are like the spirit herself: cosmic.

These Mirrors of *Sabbath Bread* are a collection, a
collage, of some of the "hows" of wisdom webbings.
Like all imaginings of spirituality, they are shared with
you in the hope that they will issue freedom and oneness with your Sacred/Creating/Relating mystery.
Through your work with them, may they lure you into
your original, virginal, natural, native gifts of the spirit.

If you are without faith-sharing companions at this
moment in your life, Mirror 1 will help you to respond
to the invitation of *Sabbath Bread.* If you belong to a
faith-sharing community you can also use the exercises
in Sample Community Sabbaths at the end of this book
to enable the community to integrate the Mirrors with
the Re-flections.

There is no linear timing demanded as "the way" in
these processes, although possible timing is suggested.
Let the webbings form, let the sabbathing space
embrace you. The spirit will challenge, lure, support,
critique, and comfort you into a Kin-dom timing. All
sabbaths provide bread. And you are always invited.

There is, however, a prerequisite. You have to
choose to wake up to the breathing of the spirit. The
choice is always yours. You have to choose to share the
bread of your sabbaths. The choice is always yours. You
have to choose to change with the ever-transforming nature of the spirit. The choice is always yours. You were
created with the breath of free will. In order to breathe
fully, you have to choose to be aware of this power to
live in constant exchange with life. May the blessings of
choice be yours!

Sabbath Bread is a guide for you to use with your
preferred journaling style. Its Re-flections are a re-

source for your *mira* collection. The Mirrors are exercises for using the book as your guide. There are also questions and suggestions that follow each Re-flection.

Whatever exercise you choose as your way of processing the Re-flections, be sure that you take time at some later moment to review, to reevaluate, and to remember the re-flections of your wisdom webbings. You will see with new vision in these reviews. There will be a deepening of your awareness of the spirit's breathing through your life. Repetition and regularity are disciplines. Both empower you to *mira* with wisdom.

Mirrors 2-8 can be used with each and all of the Re-flections. Some of the processes involve the use of your journal. But whether or not they do, after you have processed one of the exercises, record your wisdom webbings with your preferred journaling style. *Mira.*

Mirrors 9-13 are specific ways to exorcise, to release, or to be embraced by the wisdom of the Re-flections. Each process is designed for you to use in companionship with your journal, another person, or a community. *Mira.*

MIRROR 1

Journaling

Watching life, wisdom webbing, a spirituality, or whatever you name your living and breathing with the Sacred/Creating/Relating mystery, desires and requires companionship. False idols, strange gods, and/or self-deception are always possible realities for the uncompanioned sacred-searcher. Yet, each of us finds ourselves in spaces of life's webbings where we do not have the human faith companionship that we desire.

It is during these spaces that you can use a journal as a holding space or a grazing place. Your journal can be like a companion. It can be the relationship that invites you to *mira*. It can be the place where you knead the dough of your life for future bread sharing.

Journaling methods and possibilities are described in readily available published literature. If you are not familiar with any of these techniques or with the benefit of journaling, I suggest that you explore some of these resources. Perhaps you can participate in a journal workshop.

Once you have embraced a few journaling skills, you are ready to begin observing your personal style of remembering and recording life's happenings. It is important that you discover the style that is webbed with your personality, that which comes naturally to you. You want to be comfortable with this companion. You will not journal if it is an unfamiliar or strange style. "I should journal" just does not work as a motivator.

Here are some questions and suggestions that can help you to discover your journaling style:

Do you rearrange, clean, renew, or transform your appearance or environments in anticipation of another's visit? Perhaps you are someone who behaves out of the belief that when your outer environment is ordered then your inner space or feelings will follow that order. Is "ordering" your style of preparing for and recalling significant experiences? If this is one of your natural ways, then take the energy to create an ordered space for your journaling experiences, your sabbathing times.

Do you ever find yourself outwardly quiet while you are performing your daily tasks, yet at the same time there is a busy dialogue going on inwardly? Do you rehearse or replay your part in experiences by talking to yourself? Many of us do. If this is how you are, then the dialogue method of journaling may be your preferred style. In your journal, record your conversations. They will become a revealing mirror of your wisdom webbings. You may even try writing yourself or a facet of your life a letter in your journal.

Do you tell long and detailed stories when someone inquires "How are you"? Perhaps your preferred reflective style will be to pay attention to the details of your life. Record them in your journal. Which effect your behavior? What affects you: the weather? the temperature? the social events? the political tones? the religious atmosphere? relational attitudes? your body's senses? Where is your life in relationship to the patterns discovered in studies of psychology? human development? sociology? faith development? Record your observations. Look for the details of the patterns, the webbings. Each reveals a facet of the mystery of your life.

Do you gather all the facts that you possibly can before you make a decision? Then you may use your journal to record lists, collages of facets that you need to have gathered when it is time to discern that decision.

Do you sing, scream, moan, or groan as a response to a happening? Do you sulk, escape through diversion,

cry, revolt, sleep, eat, or whatever in anticipation of or
in retrospect to a significant experience? What do you
do in response to goodness? How do you behave in response to the lack of goodness? However you respond,
record your behaviors. They are your journaling
style—the way you mark life or take note of it.

A journal is one form of sabbathing, a place to record, a remembering space. It is a concrete reality. You
can write in it. You can draw in it. You can touch it,
hold, it, cry with it, pray and play with it. It is a companion. And because it is, you can even change the concept of a journal being a book into a journal being a liturgy. You can record and remember with gestures and
rituals as well as with words and pictures.

Your awareness of the breath of the spirit exchanging life with you can be ritualized by baking a cake,
throwing a party, participating in a church service,
toasting a friend, or sharing a cup, a mug, a glass, or
bread. You can ritualize wisdom's webbings by sculpting a piece of clay, or some snow or mud or sand or wood
or dough. Some of us collect pictures, match book
covers, bottles or cans, ornaments for our bodies and for
our environments, books, records, stones which are precious to us from many viewpoints, stories, jokes, pro-
verbs, quotations, notches in belts or on sticks, flowers
and/or plants. The list of how we mark what is significant to us is endless. Some of us gather vestments
like clothes, shoes, rings, pins, badges, and medals.
Some of us mark occasions with certificates, degrees,
cards, and gifts. Trees, cars, and houses can all be liturgical symbols of your life. And any of them can be your
preferred style of journaling.

Whatever your preference, choose to record your
re-flections with life so that you can *mira*. We need to
remember life's embraces, breakthroughs, breakdowns,
touches, seeming absences and alone times. It is of this
"stuff" that the spirit creates our wisdom webbings, our
spirituality. You and your journaling style can be the
eucharist of sabbath bread.

MIRROR 2

Read a Re-flection.

In your journal, list or graphically design the questions that the reading elicited within your mind.

Spend as many sabbaths as is necessary in order for you to respond to these questions. Your re-flections will be your personal imaginations of God, Jesus, church, and ministry. These are the facets of a whole spirituality.

MIRROR 3

This exercise is to be processed with the graphic that follows it. The experience can take a short or a long space of time. It is one way to get a vision of your memory, spiritual aids, present experience, future desires, and what you need, all in relationship to one of the faith mysteries of your life.

When you have completed the five parts of this exercise you will have a non-hierarchical image of one facet of your spirituality. It is very important that we image life in relationship and connections. This is the nature of the Kin-dom of God. Hierarchical imagining produces inferior and superior comparisons. We were created uniquely, not in comparison. Systems that encourage comparison and competition limit our growth as fully human creatures made in the image and likeness of the Sacred.

Now, consider one of the facets or mysteries of your spirituality. Perhaps it will be your relationship with God, or with Jesus, or with the Spirit, or with a human relationship. At another sabbath time you may repeat this with the church, prayer, etc. Once you have chosen that upon which you will focus, follow these directions:

1. What is your image of this relationship now? What is it like? Describe it to yourself. Then, in one of the spaces of the cobweb graphic, illustrate this relationship with a few adjectives, verbs, or graphic symbols.
2. What was your image of the relationship seven years or months or weeks ago? Use the number seven or one of its multiples for this

memory search. It is a number of symbolic
wholeness. What was it like? Describe it to yourself. Then, in another facet of the webbings, illustrate this memory in words or graphic symbols.
3. What or who empowered you through this
change? Or what or who supported your constan-
cy if there has been no change? What events,
happenings, insights, thoughts, or feelings effected the movement or consistency between
your response to # 1 and your response to # 2? Remember them and describe them to yourself. In
another part of the cobwebbings illustrate your
response with words or graphic symbols.
4. What do you want this relationship to be
like in the future? in seven months, weeks, or
years? Describe your hopes and desires to yourself. In another space of the cobwebbings illustrate your desired relationship with words or
graphic symbols.
5. What do you need in order that this
desired relationship may become a reality of
your spiritual life? Describe your needs to yourself. You might want to look at your responses to
#3, for often that which was of aid to you at one
time can be a clue to what you need at this time.
Illustrate your needs with words or graphic symbols on the cobwebbings.

Now, re-flect on your entire response to this exercise as you have illustrated it on the cobweb graphic.
Note the connections, the ways aspects of your relationship with this mystery connect, touch, are in tension and
challenge you. What is revealed?
    In your journal list all the questions and insights
that this re-flection issues. They will be bread for your
future sabbaths.

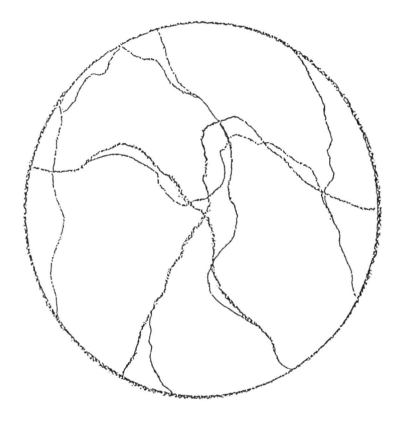

MIRROR 4

Experience a Re-flection.

Then ask yourself: What effect has this on my sacred-searching? Where does the poetry of the Re-flection web with my desires and insights? How do they influence my life responses? How is this mystery operative in my relationship with myself, others, and my God?

Record your responses to these questions with your journaling style.

MIRROR 5

These questions can be asked of each Re-flection.
Record your responses in your own journaling style.
You will be creating the webbings of your spiritual cosmos.

●What happened as I experienced this?
●What do I feel, now?
●What did I learn or relearn?
●What does it mean for my life now?

MIRROR 6

Knead some clay, or doodle while you read a Reflection of your choice. Do not concentrate on what you are molding or doodling. Just let your hands image while your eyes and mind do the reading.

When your hands seem to rest, or naturally stop their work, stop your reading. Change your mental focus. Look at what your hands have revealed as if it were a symbol.

After a comfortable space of observation and wondering, complete this sentence in your journal with 20 different responses:

This is like...

This is a way of expanding and exploring your intuitive wisdom in relationship with your mental comprehension.

MIRROR 7

Write a poem, or a story, or create a picture, a song, a sculpture, a weaving, or a dialogue with one facet from each of the Re-flections. The completion of this process can take weeks or months. You choose the timing that you need in order to be faithful to the process.

Collect all eleven of your creations in a saving place.

Repeat the entire process from the beginning.

When you have completed it the second time compare the saved collection with the just-completed one. You will notice the changes and movements of the spirit's breathing in your life.

This exercise can be repeated and the re-flection on the changes pondered as often as you find it helpful.

MIRROR 8

Explore each Re-flection, one at a time. As you do so, record all the literature that would resource the ideas and the questions that the Re-flection reveals to you.

This exercise will give you a list of books, articles, plays, records, tapes, etc. for your studying sabbaths. A topic card catalogue or a computer readout will be helpful to you.

Experience novels, poetry, folk literature, scientific studies and experiments, art, theatre, and whatever connects with the mysteries. There is no linear pattern or end to this kind of exercise. It becomes a way of *mira* living and cosmic breathing.

MIRROR 9

For Re-flecting With
"Our Need For Sabbath And Bread"

This Re-flection invites you to choose sabbathing as
a spiritual exercise for your sacred-searching discipline. By example, it illustrates some of the nourishment, the bread that sabbathing will issue in and
through your awareness. It sets the re-flective, the *mira*,
atmosphere for you to bring to the rest of the Re-
flections. It also illustrates a way of recording the happenings within a sabbath space and a way to let your recordings issue questions. If you respond "Yes" to this
invitation to regular sabbathing you can use each of the
Re-flections as a guide for your sabbath space experiences.

The process that this Re-flection models for you can
be repeated and re-repeated. If you are faithful to your
intentions, attention and work, your re-flections will reveal a pattern. Perhaps it will look like a dance, or a
map with directions, or a webbing. Whatever the pattern, it will re-flect your ever-flowing relationship with
the Sacred Mystery of Life: God.

Faithfulness and work are required. Spiritual
awareness cannot be had from any "Instant Shop." You
need to covenant your time and space of sabbathing.
This promise or covenant will call you to faithfulness.
Be realistic about your timing. A sabbath space of fif-
teen minutes a day, or one hour a week, or a day a
month can each nourish you with the bread of wisdom.
What is important is that you keep your commitment,
and you cannot do so if your covenant is made unrealis-

tically. Choose your time for sabbathing out of a sense of your total relational life and responsibilities. The choice is yours. Do not make a promise out of your own or others' expectations. And remember that faithfulness is not to be judged by successes but in relationship with the fruits of the spirit and your desire for freedom and oneness with the Holy.

Mira!

MIRROR 10

For Re-flecting With "The Kin-dom"

This Re-flection is a playful prayer with a few of the parables of Jesus as they are recorded in Luke's gospel. Prayer and play require the same inter-webbing of risk and trust. For example, we cannot program true humor or a game. We enter the experience of it. Then we re-flect upon the experience and see that a plan was operative. We had to risk our own contribution in the experience and we had to trust another's contribution. Both prayer and play are intimate, up front, expressions of ourselves at the moment of the interaction. Sometimes we learn to pray in and through our play.

Play with some of the parables of Jesus. Remember that the parables are always about the Kin-dom and its way of knowing life and relationships. As it was for the original hearers of the parables, so it is with us: We do not expect what they reveal. Each parable is about the Kin-dom that is both now and yet to come.

Ask yourself: What does this parable re-flect? What does it reveal? Do not dismiss thoughts or insights that come to you just because you have never heard anyone else say it. The spirit can reveal the meaning of the scriptures to you as well as to anyone else. Record your vision, your wisdom revelations.

After praying with and recording several parable revelations, try webbing them into an original or personal expression in story, through poetry or with a picture. This playing process will reveal more facets of the Kin-dom to you. It will become a mirror that will confirm and critique your values and behaviors in relationship to the Kin-dom's Ways.

MIRROR 11

For Re-flecting With "Watch Life"

Choose a sabbath day in which you will have the time and space to watch your life in the style of this Reflection. Plan your day:

- eight hours for sleep and rest,
- eight hours for refreshment and nourishment of your mind, body and spirit,
- eight hours for your wisdom work.

Once you have made the choice of a day and set this pattern for yourself you will need to design just how you will spend your eight hours of wisdom work. Here is a possible model.

Become still by quieting yourself with music, a relaxation exercise, a chant, a humming sound, or simply by paying attention to the rhythm of your breathing. When you feel that you are sufficiently stilled, give thanks and praise to the Holy of your life for the possibility and gift of this time and space.

Ask for awareness, for alertness, and for the grace of an active imagination. In the act of asking the spirit for your needs, you are both naming yourself in relationship with the power that can fund you with the grace you need and preparing yourself to receive what you name in the asking.

Look into the mirror of your life. *Mira.* Keep watching, in your preferred style, until an experience, event, feeling, conversation, or relationship becomes clearly present to you. Then, recall its beginning, middle, and end. Tell yourself the story of this life revelation.

Ask yourself: How would I image, or what sense do I have, or how do I think about or value this remembered happening? How would I describe it or illustrate it as it webs with my relationship with God? Let your preferred recalling style do the work for you. Do not rush or push the time this takes. Let it flow from you. You have asked for this grace. Receive it graciously.

(You may desire a break for refreshment or nourishment at this point. You choose.)

When you feel ready, record the fruit of your watching thus far. Do so in writing, drawing, ritual, song, sculpting, or whatever you desire. Take your time!

(This is another possible space in the process for you to break, if you so desire.)

Ask yourself how this recorded image re-flects your values. Or how it challenges your values in life. Think about how renewed or new values would effect your behaviors. Remember your daily relationships and commitments to yourself, with others and with your God. Be specific and concrete.

Record your responses.

(If you have not taken a space for refreshment or nourishment up until this point in the process, do so now. You will need the energy that such bread provides when you give your full attention to the rest of this process.)

Review the wisdom webbings of your "watching life" work up to this moment. Be still and gather your sense of the experience. These questions can focus you:

● What happened?
● What do I feel?

● What have I learned or relearned?
● What can this possibly mean for my life now?

When you have thought about your response to one or all of these questions, record your responses.

Conclude this process of "watching life" with a prayer of praise and thanksgiving to the Holy of your life.

This type of exercise can be repeated several times during your sabbath day. Or it may be the one process you use throughout your eight hours of wisdom-webbing work. If so, you can repeat the process the next day, if you are on retreat, or the next time you have a day for sabbathing. If you re-flect with this process often enough, it will become a natural way for you to watch your life.

Another name to give this kind of re-flective exercise is "awareness examination" or "examination of consciousness." It is a way to discern the workings of the spirit in, through and with your ordinary, daily life experiences. The happenings of your life, your memories of them, and your reevaluation of them in the breath and light of the spirit, is the "stuff" from which a wisdom spirituality is created.

Postscript:

If you can become aware of balancing each day of your life on an "8-8-8" hour pattern, you will also experience holistic health. Your body is naturally balanced in this timing: eight hours for each of the bodily functions of ingestion, digestion, and elimination. Webbing your body functions and your spiritual awareness will issue greater harmony. Such an ordering is re-flective of your Kin-dom-created goodness.

MIRROR 12

For Re-flecting With
"Communions of the Kin-dom"

Read this Re-flection.

Name five, six, or as many as you can of the questions that the reading issues in your mind. Record them.

Write, draw, paint, sculpt, whittle, weave, knead, construct, or think about an image that responds to one or more of the questions.

Since this Re-flection is about sharing such bread as you have just made, share your questions and imaged responses with another person. You can do this through verbal conversation or in a letter. Sometimes the phone is a media for sharing.

After the sharing, record your experience of this communion.

MIRROR 13

For Re-flecting With
"Imaging the Sacred,"
"Our Vision of Prayer,"
"Incarnation,"
"Jesus,"
"The Paschal Event,"
"Becoming Church," and
"Conversion Toward Originality"

These Re-flections can be a guide for your spiritual
direction in any order that you may choose. Each one is
followed by questions and suggestions that will help you
to process the wisdom. Take as much time with each
one as you desire or require in order to deepen your
relationship with the mystery. Do not compare your timing with anyone else's timing. The spirit will breathe
originally and individually within you.

With your preferred remembering style, record
your wisdom in relationship to each of the Re-flections.
Some of Mirrors 2-8 suggest ways for you to do this.
And in the section that follows the Re-flections, that
is in Sample Community Sabbaths, you can find other
suggestions that may web with your style of response.

Whatever way you choose to pray with these
wisdom-webbing expressions, be blessed with the
peaceful awareness that you will be breathing with the
spirit. Your spirituality will be deepening. Your imaginations of and responses to the mysteries of the
Christian faith will affect other companions on the
earth. Sabbathing individuals and communities are a
revelation of the Kin-dom of God.

II.
THE
RE-FLECTIONS

RE-FLECTION 1

 Our Need For Sabbath And Bread

It is 6:30 A.M. EST.

I am sitting alone with the ocean. All my senses are alert to and intuitively enraptured with a "knowing" that seems to be both within and beyond me. Wonders well deep in me as we exchange breath. I want to share this, now, with all my friends: with creation itself. Then, absent loves break as waves and companion my experiences with their remembered presence. I am stilled with the wonder of the sea.

Do others somehow know that they are with me?

How can I let them know?

Why do I desire to be with them and to be alone, all at the same time?

Is this what I mean to ask for when I pray: Give us this day our daily bread?

I pray:

God, Companion with all creation,
We are your kin in need of bread for life.

Give us who hunger for food, bread for our bodies.
Give us who hunger for courage, bread for our spirits.
Give us who hunger for compassion, bread for our hearts.

Be our nourishment as we share our hands, our

food, and our love among our kin.

And may the Kin-dom come among us, as it is with you, now and forever.

Amen.

The questions continue to ride the ocean's surf. Like the surf they also seem both before and within me. Dawn has deepened into morning. The beach is now alive with other people. I watch and wonder: Are these people, too, communing with intuitive companions? Are we ever really alone? Are we always really alone?

Stillness overwhelms me again. I am nowhere and everywhere all at once...all at one...all is one. Then I remember that I had been tossing during the night before this morning. I tossed, not with the sea, but with a sense of readying for dawn. Twilight seemed to have been breathing its coming. Yet I am not exhausted. Rather, I am refreshed. Wonder washes in a new revelation like another wave of knowing: This is sabbath!

SABBATH...

timeless time
spaceless space
both and
an alone togetherness
a breathing breathlessness
a multi-faceted oneness
an intuitive knowing

SABBATH...

Come away awhile.
Be still.
Take, eat and remember.
Follow me.
Know.
Listen.

Look.
Mira.
Know that I AM holy.
Breathe deeply.
Watch and wait.
Now.

SABBATH...

sacred-searching
wisdom webbing
ordinarily extra-ordinary
extra-ordinarily ordinary
holy now
all who come are invited to eat
come
embrace
enjoy
celebrate

Like all treasures, sabbath has its price. The cost is time and space. We, however, are time-and-space captives. Sabbath is an invitation to break the bindings. It is a call from slavery to freedom. But how often is our response to this lure a further enslavement: "I have no time. I'm in a hurry"? And so we eat fast foods and wonder why we are still hungry. We snatch winks and wonder why we are not refreshed. We work without imagination and wonder why we are uninspired. We never stop. We turn constantly and wonder why we are dizzy.

One of my wisdom books, *What To Do If You're Afraid Of The Dark* (Green Tiger Press, 1979) says: "If the clock stops...use your own hands to tell time." Our hands are a true telling of time. Try stopping your hands for a sabbath space. Notice that time is not lost but gained! Try it. Turn off the lights in your home or work space for just one day. Live with the timing of nature's light and darkness. Watch how your own hands, your own eyes, your whole being, when in tune with nature, knows the time that is *now*.

In wisdom's ways, time is infinitely now and space is everywhere here. Wisdom's friends, like Jesus, chose to respond to the bidding of sabbath. They lived with a plurality of possibilities and a multitude of imaginations. No wonder wise ones have followers, disciples. We all long to be wisdom's disciples. We know that we have become impoverished without her. We lack imagination, intuition, and possibilities. We have chosen slavery rather than sabbath. We have forgotten the story of freedom. But, earth's prophets, like Jesus, inspire us with sabbath invitations: Look! *Mira!* Be alert! Wake up! The time is now!

What are we to wake up to? Perhaps to the graciousness of all of creation as it mirrors its creator. Graciousness is like all of life exchanging breath. Through the exchange, all is connected and related to all. There is abundance, grace. Such an awareness will issue a trust of life rather than a grasping at life.

Perhaps we are to wake up to the passion of life lived in such a constant exchange. "Compassion" means to be passionate, full of life, with another. It means to breathe the truth of ourselves and each creature. With a compassionate awareness, we come to know that all life is both amazingly different, that is differently abled, and totally bonded in the webbings of companionship. What a miracle we see in the mirror of such *Mira*.

Mira (Spanish for "look") is the poetic root, the inner core, of all experiences with mirrors and miracles. To see another possibility is a miracle. To look at life with eyes hoping for relationship is to see life reflecting the harmony of the creator. Sabbath is a *mira* experience of time and space. Through a sabbath we can see, as if in a re-flection, that all of life is webbings of differently abled creatures breathing in harmony.

The need for sabbath time and space is a natural desire. We are as hungry for sabbath as we are hungry for "bread." The fruits of our sabbathing experiences, in truth, do feed us. The bread is multi-grained. And it is

for the feeding of others who are hungry, our kin of the
earth, the kin of the Kin-dom. The bread that issues
from our sabbaths is the daily bread we naturally
desire.

What will this daily bread look like? We know that
bread is often a loaf of baked meal, salt, water, and
leaven. These ingredients, in bonding with many other
enrichments, give us many possibilities: all bread.
However, the touching of our bodies and breaths, and
the exchange of natural and sacred desires, can also be
bread. The sharing of our breaking and healing hearts
can be bread. Once I broke black bread with sacred-
searching peoples as we were remembering our exodus
events. My hunger for journeying companions was fed
beyond expectations. We can all feast, and fast, with the
bread of life. We will find that we will not go hungry.
The miracle is that there is always enough bread when
we feed one another. And bread has as many shapes
and forms as sacred-searching peoples can knead into
sharing.

Let me feed your imagination with some of the
bread possibilities that have nourished my life:

I gather weekly with women with whom I share
community. We come together to break the bread of a
scripture/story. This "corporate scripture sharing" is a
sabbath space for our natural community growth. One
among us gathers the rest of us and the word, all ingredients of the bread, with a prayer for insight and a
telling of a story from the scriptures. Then we sit, alone
yet together, in our solitude spaces re-flecting on the
reading as if it were a mirror for our life. We may remain in this sacred-searching circle, each looking in silence, for twenty to thirty minutes. Then each of us, in
turn, tells the story of what the mirror of words re-
flected for her. The shared word is bread for the life of
our sistering love. This we share daily with each other
and those our work embraces. We conclude with one
among us verbalizing a prayer that gathers the concerns
and thanksgivings of the group.

On one such sabbath experience, our community read the story of Mary and Martha sending for Jesus because their brother, Lazarus, was dying (Jn. 11). The story related that when Jesus heard the news, he cried. Later, Mary and Martha cried because Lazarus had died and Jesus still had not arrived. Then the scene presented the hired mourners, as well as neighbors and friends, who cried.

As I looked into the mirror of this story I saw myself crying. I re-flected on all the ways and whys that release my tears: loss; fear; pain; being overwhelmed; at comings and goings of friends and life's events; when caught in the wonder of love or the lack of love; through laughter; when reconciled; in consolation; in desolation; in the midst of an embrace; during births, baptisms, and deaths; on the edges of breakdowns or breakthroughs; during newscasts and movies; with clowns; with any tenderness I encounter; and so many more. Tears of many possibilities. I also saw in this mirror all the earth's kin, my brothers and sisters, crying for the ways and whys of their lives.

In this mirror I remembered a truth that a lecture, another form of a sabbath space, revealed to me. The speaker told the story of the earth's crust and its presentation of itself as a water planet. She said that the crust of the earth is 71 percent salt water. This memory connected me with the facet of knowledge that says that each human's body is 71 percent salt water. Tears came to my eyes with this sabbath bread realization of kinship.

No matter the reasons, or the geography that may distance us, or the language or skin or values or rituals that may seem to make us so different and separate from one another, we all cry the same tears; the tears of our mother the earth. When I cry because of loss, I taste the salt water of the planet and her kin. And it is the same salt water that drenches the broken yet hopeful hearts of peoples in Harlem, Up-town, and South Africa. It is the same salt water of the kin of Russia,

Brazil, Indonesia and Central America. No wonder, I re-flected, all peoples have and continue to worship and initiate new kin with the harmony of salt and water. It is natural. It is a virginal instinct. Salt water is a sacred symbol by which we name, claim, and proclaim our companionship with all and with the Holy of all.

The *mira* wisdom of this sabbath experience challenged and enlightened me with other webbings:

> And if salt loses its flavor?
> Go to the storehouse of relationship, of kin-dom values, where your tears and the tears of others will wash you clean.
> Your tears of truth will set you free.
> Heal and be made whole.
> Lazarus, come forth!

That sabbath space of sacred-searching fed me beyond my expectations. Now, every time I well up with tears, I taste the bread of companionship. I remember that the word "companion" means to share bread with another. And I have a deeper bond with those who also cry. We are kin. Our tears bond the grains of our lives into bread, and we eat and remember.

Another *mira* revelation occurred when a group of my friends gathered with me to make bread. We collected ourselves and the necessary ingredients and utensils. We watched, with attention, as the different flours, the oil, the honey, the salt, the water, and the leaven each touched and embraced each other until they became the harmony of dough. Then we kneaded the dough.

Each of us kneaded the dough. We held it, caressed it, stretched it and challenged it into more than just the separate ingredients. We also shared with each other what we saw as we looked into the process of bread making. We looked into it as a mirror for our lives. Then we molded it into a loaf and baked it. While it was baking and we were waiting, we continued to share stories of other waiting and baking times of our lives.

Later, when we ate the bread in thanksgiving and
worship, we shared much more than ingredients
kneaded into dough and baked into bread. We ate from
the loaf of shared lives. It had been leavened with our
wisdom. Our tears had bonded us. Bread making had
indeed become a miracle. We shared the sacredness of
sabbath bread.

We all need to be fed such nourishment. We need
sabbath. We need bread. "The Kin-dom of God is like a
woman who put leaven into three measures of flour."
(Lk. 13) How much flour do we need to gather? How
many hands are needed to knead the dough into bread?
How many stories can be shared during the waiting, the
baking time? How many are to be invited to the sabbath
sharing? What size and shape will the table need to be
in order to welcome all who respond to the invitation?
When will this sabbath bread be ready to serve? How
will we express our gratitude? Eucharist! *Gracias!*

Come!

Mira!

The Kin-dom of God is now!

SABBATH BREAD...

we hunger
daily
eat
remember
sabbath
bread

Questions and Suggestions for Re-flection

● During what experiences or at what times of
your life do you remember yourself crying out a desire
for time and space?

● Remember. Observe. *Mira*. These are clues for
you about your need and times for sabbath.

● Begin to observe your daily and weekly routine
in order to choose your sabbath possibilities. Then set
the time and space aside as your sabbath.

● Jesus referred to himself as the Bread of Life.
The gospels are mirrors where we can taste this bread.
During your sabbath space try to respond to some of
these questions which the Gospel of John re-flects to us:

> Who are you?
> Are you a prophet?
> How do you know me?
> How can a person be born when old?
> Can one enter a second time into the
> mother's womb?
> Where do you get that living water? bread of
> life?
> What do you want?
> Do you want to be healed? to be fed the bread
> of life?

RE-FLECTION 2

 The Kin-dom Of God Is Like...

Where does the desire to gather and share the bread of life come from? Within? Beyond? The realm of the deep? The kin? The Other? From the Kin-dom of God!

To what can this Kin-dom be compared?

Mira!

Look into the mirror of Luke's stories as re-flected in Chapters 13 and 15 of his memory of the Christ events.

Wonder with me.

The Kin-dom of God is like...

A woman
who lives from day to day
as if life were an ever-flowing river,
babbling and bubbling: I AM WHO I AM.
She trusts life to issue
all that is needed
in order to live
wholly.
The I AM
of her inner core
is leaven,
enough for daily bread.

She is enough!
Each breath of life
is a kneading
of the loaf
of now.
And with the abundance
of enough
the lady shares
life
with the companions
the day
gathers.

She is gracious
and compassionate,
breathing harmony
with all of life.

Today,
from the midst
of life's constant exchange
of comings and goings,
her intuition remembers,
breathes,
a deep-flowing wisdom,
an almost lost story.
Woman,
this lady,
comes alive
with its memory...

Her grandparents were shepherds. She had seen
pictures of them in the faded family album. That album
held pictures of the dog, of the sheep and of the pastures and their home. There were even pictures of the
exchange of wool with the buyers, for her grandparents
were well praised by their work, and people
everywhere desired the rich fruits of such pride.
Grandpa also loved to watch the sheep. Somehow
each one seemed to image something different, something very special about itself. He watched and
watched. And he breathed with the ways of their lives

as if he were re-flecting in a mirror. This mirror spoke to him. It uttered a wisdom message: All creation is differently abled! Grandpa would watch, and then he'd tell the tales of these sheep to Grandma.

And Grandma loved to listen to Grandpa, breathing his stories into the dough she kneaded. For Grandma delighted in making bread. Somehow each touch of the leavened measures was an embrace, an enabling, a challenging of the dough into more. Bread making whispered its rising wisdom: Life always is more than expected.

Yes, sheep and bread directed all of Grandpa's and Grandma's lives. Together they breathed their companions' wisdom: I am who I am and I am enough! God's presence dwelt in their midst.

Today,
NOW,
the woman remembers
this almost lost story.
It's wisdom
flows through her being
as Grandma's words
breathe
in her memory...

"One day Grandpa couldn't be still. Somehow one of the sheep was missing from the flock. The feeling of absence was like a wild storm within him. When it finally deluged he thundered, 'I must go find the lost one.'

"So Grandpa left the ordinary ways of the days: the walking and the watching, the shearing, the exchange with the buyers, the storytelling with me, watching me make bread, and the sharing of our lives and the sharing of bread with others. All had to wait while he went in search of the lost one.

"Waiting wasn't acceptable to others. They gasped and grasped:
  'How can you go now? I'm here to buy.'
  'Your timing isn't right for me!'

'If you leave now, I'll go elsewhere to spend my money. And I'll never come back here!'

Their threats were warnings to Grandpa, and to me, that his choice would definitely issue changed life.

"For three days I kneaded bread. I breathed my wonder and worry into that dough. Within myself I knew that this time, like all of life, would issue more than expected.

"However, others were not as hopeful. They spread the word that the business was finished. They said that it had folded because the silly man had gone off looking for one of the sheep and forgetting all that was important in life.

"But, you see, Grandpa hadn't been forgetting anything. He was, instead, remembering it all. Each moment of those three days he watched all the other sheep. He knew the wisdom of each one's specialness and difference. As he breathed with this knowing, the uniqueness of the almost lost one was revealed. And then he knew exactly where to find it.

"When he freed her from the enslaving thorn bush near the ever-flowing river, which was always babbling and bubbling its truth, Grandpa held her close and calmed her fear. After awhile he carried her back to the flock.

"No one, except me, noticed Grandpa's return. But as soon as I saw him I went out to the pasture to be with him. I held him. Together, Grandpa and I, just stood and watched all the sheep.

"To celebrate the return of Grandpa and the almost lost sheep, we planned a feast. We sent out invitations to everyone. I remember them well! They read:

The Lady And Lord of Sabbath Pastures
Invite You
to Celebrate
What Watching Life Reveals!
Bread Will Be Served.
Come.
All Welcome.
All the Time.

Yes,
the lady of the kin-dom
of daily living
had heard
this story
often
as a child.
But, today,
it is new.
This almost lost story,
newly kneaded,
is now known
as the inner core
of her own life's wisdom.

And this wisdom
breathes:
The kin-dom comes
with
watching life.
All that you need
to live life
wholly,
holy,
will be revealed
moment
by
moment.
Add
the leaven of your breath
to the abundance.
Then share
the more than expected
with whomever
the moment gathers.

So, today,
the Kin-dom lady
of daily living
issues

invitations
to all
who have eyes to see,
to all
who have ears to hear,
to all
who have meal to share,
to all
who have stories to remember:

The Kin of the Kin-dom
Invites You to the Sabbath.
Celebrate What Remembering Life Reveals.
Come.
Bread Will Be Served.
All Welcome.
All the Time.

Questions and Suggestions for Re-flection

● This Re-flection was issued from a series of questions that I asked about the Kin-dom of God in relationship to some gospel parables. Read a parable and in
your journal list all the questions that it issues.

● Ponder some of these questions of Matthew's gospel:

   If salt looses its flavor can it become salty again?
   Do you light a lamp and put it under a bushel
   basket?
   Isn't life worth more than food?
   Isn't the body worth more than clothes?
   Aren't you worth more than the birds and flowers?
   Why are you so frightened?
   Are you the one or are we to look for someone else?
   What did you expect to see?
   To what can I compare the kin-dom to today?

RE-FLECTION 3

Watch Life

The story of the previous Re-flection is a webbing of some of the "stuff" that was moving in my imagination over that last few years as I prayed with the parables. I would read a gospel parable and ask two questions: What does this parable reveal about the Kindom of God? What facets of my life, what images, what values, what behaviors, does it challenge? And after awhile, the responses that these questions issued began to look like cobwebbings. As I stayed with this image, it gradually issued the story.

I have learned this way to pay attention, to be alert, through an experience I had had with a retreat director as I was completing a six-month journey with the *Spiritual Exercises* of St. Ignatius of Loyola. Because of that experience, and my faithfulness to the Exercises, I had been feeling an enormous sense of freedom and power in my spiritual life. A part of me wanted to build a tent and stay, a sentiment not unlike Peter's after he experienced the Transfiguration of Christ. Yet there was another part of me that wanted to run out and share my freed spirit with the whole world. It was a feeling of wanting to be both a cloistered hermit and a mendicant preacher, all at the same time.

I had been so sure that the only reason for this energy, this grace, was because I had been faithful to the patterned discipline of the Spiritual Exercises. I had practiced the wisdom of repetition. I had allowed myself to be guided by both the director and the Exercises. Thus it was, with all my surety and enthusiasm, that I asked the director to give me a new set of exercises. I wanted a new discipline that would keep this freedom alive for "the rest of my life"!

"Georgene," she responded, "watch life."

Now, I was intending to do this. But why wasn't she understanding that what I wanted was a new guide? Well, I had exaggerated a bit. I knew that nothing would really last the rest of my life. So, I repeated my request for something that would keep me free until my next year's retreat.

"Georgene," she responded, "watch life." And she repeated this when I again formed the request within the limits of what pattern I was to follow until our next spiritual direction session.

I went home with wonder, disappointment, and resolve. Why, after six months of companioning me, couldn't she understand what it was that I was requesting? Hadn't I been clear in how I was saying it? Perhaps I hadn't been intense enough about my deep sense of freedom. Whatever, I knew that "I knew" what I was looking for. I would return the next month with the treasure and surprise her.

"WATCH LIFE!" Her repeated response haunted me daily. It became like a never-ending chant that echoed within me each time I breathed. More questions began to web their ways into my days and nights. Watch life? Was I watching? What was I watching? Whose life? How did my watching and living touch other life? How would this issue freedom? Was I in control of my life? Was any life mine to control? How could I learn to embrace life? to enjoy life? to suffer life? How could I watch life and not grasp at it?

"WATCH LIFE!" From somewhere in the midst of all the questioning and resolve, the wisdom of these words became apparent. I remembered that it was because I was watching life that I had known when to seek out a director for the Spiritual Exercises. And it was because of what I was watching and how I was watching

that the Holy was revealed in and through my life. Life
was where I had come to know and be known. Life was
the mirror I was to watch for the continuing revelation
of the Sacred.

   With this realization, gratitude deepened within
me. I was thankful that the director had really known
what I was asking for. And I came to appreciate the
power of the midwife, the person who can pay attention
to the movements of the birthing of the spirit from
another's life. The midwife knows that the life being issued is not her or his own life. Yet, the midwife knows
that it is the watching of life with wisdom that truly
companions the new life to fullness and to freedom. My
director and her words "watch life" were the midwife,
the pattern, the power for which I was searching.

   Since that experience I have regularly chosen time
and space to sabbath with "Watch Life." I sit with
whatever life the spirit re-flects to me. I ask questions
about what I am looking at. The following are some
stories from my own sabbath spaces. I share them with
the hope that some facet or particle of their webbings
will lure you to "Watch Life."

   I sat quietly. I breathed easily and with awareness.
And all the while I asked myself: What do I sense as I
watch my life at this time? I waited, paying attention to
a whole strain of thoughts and images. What finally
stayed with me was a picture or sense of myself stand-
ing on the edge of a precipice. I felt scared. The darkness before me was blinding and deep. I glanced behind
myself. It was the same. I was on the edge of darkness
and fear. I was terrified that I would fall or be pushed
over the edge. There seemed to be a presence somewhere. What was it going to do to me?

   This image stayed with me for several months of
sabbath times. It was not comforting. But, then, neither
were the experiences of my lived reality. I was in a
transitional period of life. I had just severed a covenant

with one community and had committed myself in covenant to another community. I was trying to trust the new covenant relationship. On some days I felt divorced from all of life. On other days I felt near death. And yet, on other days I had a renewed sense of the power and grace of my choice.

In my life, as in the imagining I do during my sabbaths, I kept turning around, very cautiously checking out what was before and behind me. One sabbath, as I looked, I saw a spark, a bit of light. Perhaps this image was issued from a touch of love from my daily living experiences. Whatever its source, its reality was present and gave me hope for continuing my watching, my sabbaths. Then...

One sabbath space I sensed myself on the edge of a precipice. However, all was light! There was light before me and behind me. I turned cautiously, but with sight. Within myself I felt a wild surprise. I looked over the precipice and saw below me a valley luscious with life. What I experienced was abundant life: more than expected. Then I realized that what was before me was only the re-flections of what was behind me. This was a comforting gift. I was grateful for the change the constant turning had issued. It was a conversion.

Part of the gift was the realization that I was to walk and live in the valley. The time was coming. And I would not walk alone. For now I was to wait with hope. I was to trust life as I experienced it now. It, too, was a gift.

The fruit of this new vision was harvested in my relational life. I became more trusting of the processes and the timing of the transitions in my life. I was less edgy as I related with others. I watched all of life with a renewed sense of hope and trust.

"Where am I in my relationship with God these days?" I asked myself during one sabbath time. I sat and waited for a response. My imagination issued this:

First I sensed that I was floating. Then I felt an embrace. Slowly the image cleared and I realized that I was being carried under the wing of a mother bird. We were soaring over a valley abundant with life. I would soon be walking in that valley.

The image left me, but a sense of my God's love remained. I came to a renewed understanding of the truth that I have been given all the power or grace that I will need in life. I was actually being carried by graciousness. If I would faithfully live with this truth, I would always be at the right place at the right time. And it wouldn't matter whether I was soaring above it or walking in the valley of life.

I went into a retreat experience asking myself what I wanted this time away to issue in my life. The desire that came to me was for wisdom. I needed to know how to be faithful to the gospel in my new job. I had just accepted the invitation to companion the novices of our community as their director. I knew that I would have to pay attention to the now as well as to the new. I would have to be faithful to history and to prophecy. How could I web all of this into an experience for the novices that would be a gospel re-flection of the Kin-dom of God?

The retreat concluded and the gift I asked for was granted. I had received the wisdom to know that I would not do this job alone. Most of the work would be the power of the spirit. The spirit would be the director. I was to pay attention to the movements of the spirit in my life and in the lives of those I would companion.

I boarded the plane and focused my attention on the return trip. Somewhere, between then and not-yet-home, I began to experience an uneasiness in my gut. Was this anxiety over the flight? Over the new job? Why was the peacefulness of the retreat gone so soon? What was going on? Why these butterflies in my heart? I sat back, breathed deeply and tried to let my imagination do the work of responding to all the questions.

An image did appear. I saw myself with my two

hands outstretched in front of me. They were holding a yellow object. What was it? It seemed very fragile. It also seemed to contain all of life's gifts. But I was holding it! Then I knew that it was an egg yolk. There was no shell, yet the yolk remained whole.

I sensed that that was indeed how I was to be as a novice director—as a person who companions others in their sacred-searching. I was to hold all of life and its gifts out in front of me. I was to remember that I was not the giver; rather I was to be the revealer or the midwife of the gifts from others' lives. The peace of the retreat returned. The new insight and image helped me to treasure wisdom's gifts even more. As the flight ended and I left the plane a new question arose: Who would be the first person to break my yolk?

I walked with the gift of this image and that final question for days, maybe it was weeks. I was very protective of that wisdom and of the image. Of course I told no one. When I was asked about my retreat I would simply report that it was very revealing and that its goodness still held me. But I would walk away wondering if that person had seen "my gift," or if she or he was the one who would poke their finger into "my yolk."

I cannot remember just what woke me up. It might have been only when I realized that the yolk was indeed running all over my hands and life! Or perhaps it was when I came to realize that others were guarding themselves from me. Whatever it was, it shouted at me: "*Mira!* Look at what you are doing."

I looked into the mirror of the image of my hands carrying the yolk. I was grasping that yolk, that image, the gift of its revelation. I was the first person who had poked her finger into the yolk and I had done so the moment I began to protect the gift.

I let go. I remembered that as the gift had been freely given to me so I was to give it to others. I knew in a deeper way the wisdom of knowing how to embrace life without grasping at it. I prayed to stay awake to this wisdom.

Once, in the middle of life and one of its hard spots, I cried out: "All right, I'll carry this burden. But who will take care of me?" The response echoed from deep within me, from a hollow space of sacred presence: "I will."

I wanted to remember this comfort. So I scribbled the revelation on an already used piece of paper that I had in my coat pocket. When I got home I put the paper on my desk. Its message and memory carried me through many burdens.

Sometime later, a friend gave me a rock from Mt. Sinai. He hoped that it would be a symbol of an aged covenant and give me strength. I received the rock and the hope, and I wrote "I Will" on it to remind me of a personal covenant. The rock, the question, the message, and the friend all remain mirrors for me. In them I see the promise and faithfulness of the Sacred as it breathes in my life.

A mermaid, a servant of the watery depths, once played the role of a mirror for my sacred-searching. She took the time to go down to the bottom of the sea, and resting in its bed, she listened to the core of the earth. She taught me that, like all mermaids, I cannot be raped when I am listening, obedient, to the Core of Life: the Sacred/Creating/Relating mystery.

During some winter months a few moons ago, I chose to take a space away from the familiar. As I was treasuring this solitude, my imagination burned with questions: Who are you, O Holy One? What can I name you? How are we related? How can I name myself in this relationship? The lights of these fires accompanied my eating, walking, sleeping, and wondering. Each day I share the experiences of these fires with a retreat direc-

tor, for I knew that conversion is best recognized in the
mirror of conversation. There one can see herself, "turn
with" (con-vert), the covenanting God.

One of the instruments of expression that I had
brought with me to this sabbath space was a set of water
colors. I had no plans or, for that matter, any real talent.
But I knew that there are times in the inner work experience when a non-verbal expression is necessary in
order to see more clearly what is being revealed.

Thus it was that one morning I used the water
colors and let the inspirations as well as the paints flow
from me to the paper. There was a kind of abandonment
about the experience. I painted whatever came. When I
felt finished I looked at what was there. It seemed to resemble a lot of flames clustered together. I left the image for a few hours. When I returned to the image I
brushed it with the color brown, encaving the clustered
fires. Even later that day, I took the color green and
made what looked like a webbing under the flames.
And, again, I went away from the image for a few hours.

That evening I sat with the painting, looking into it
as if it were a mirror. I hoped that it would reflect some
truth to me. As I looked, all my previous questions returned. I sat for quite some time with this "picture" and
with the questions breathing in me.

As I was about to conclude that evening's meditation period a story and an affirmation seemed to appear
in my mirror. I remembered the tale of Moses' encounter with fire and questions. He had discovered who he
was in that experience. Then, fearful of the mission that
this new identity was demanding, Moses begged for the
experience to reveal its name. He knew that he needed
to rely on some power other than his own if he was to
fulfill the vocation that the experience was issuing. And
a "talking, burning bush" just didn't seem to convey any
of what was needed! His plea was answered with an
ever-flowing name: "I am who I am who I am who...It is
Yahweh who speaks."

From within my memory of this ancient story, there

seemed to flow out an affirming, loving response to all my questions. What I experienced was a power telling me that I was all that I was at that moment. And I was good enough. I couldn't create myself to be any more. I was all that the Sacred/Creating/Relating mystery had issued thus far. An enormous sense of peace and comfort embraced me with the words: "Georgene, you are who you are and you are enough."

Such an experience needs to be recorded so that one can remember it when neither comfort nor affirmation are present. So I took my pencil and wrote those words right on the painting. Or, so I thought I did. When I sat back down and looked at it I realized that I had written: "I am who I am and I am enough."

These words, issued from the entire experience, still remain as an embrace and a mission from the Holy for my daily living. The creating God, the empowering Sacred, the transforming Holy is with me. I am not alone. Yahweh's name is I Am Who I Am. My relationship with the Holy is named I Am Who I Am And I Am Enough.

●●●

Several sabbath experiences ago, I was guided through a meditation entitled "The Wise Person." During that fantasy it was suggested that I journey to a cave where I would encounter a person who would symbolize wisdom for my life. Through my imagination I was invited to converse with the wise one. Then, when I was about to leave the cave, the wisdom figure gave me a gift to symbolize my own wisdom. Even within this fantasy I was surprised by the gift I received. It was a cotton ball. Then the guided meditation concluded. In my outer reality I tried to contemplate the meaning of this gift.

Well, a cotton ball!? So I had a softness about myself. Or at least I desired such wisdom. But this ball of cotton was virgin cotton! It was newly plucked from its mother plant. It still held seeds in its gentle yet firm

embrace. Its fibers were a tight webbing. Everything
was touching, was connecting with all else. How could I
be like such virgin cotton?

Some sabbaths later I reconsidered this image. I
pondered the meaning of "virgin." I questioned the mirror of this virgin cotton ball about some of its charac-
teristics. I wondered why it is that we name some
people "virgins." I had a hunch that we don't really
mean that they are just genitally virgins. I looked at
people like Mary of Nazareth, John the Baptist, Mary of
Bethany, and Jesus himself. What did their stories have
to do with my search for wisdom?

I went to the gospel/mirror of Matthew and read
the parable of the Wise Virgins (Mt. 25). I read the story
several times. I also remembered a description of a virgin that I had read somewhere else. The essence of that
description was that a virgin is a person who lives life
by interdependently relating with every creature that
she or he encounters. But the virgin only roots her or his
identity — is only dependently related — to One. That
One is the ground and source of all being. I interpreted
that to mean that a virgin is one who breathes in relationship with all of creation, but knows that the source
of breath itself is the Sacred/Creating/Relating mystery
we name God.

Well, that is quite an identity! Its freedom and re-
sponsibility demand both trust and abandonment. All of
this was shedding some light on my gift of a virgin cotton
ball as a symbol of wisdom.

I reread the gospel parable. Why were some of
these virgins named wise and some not so wise: fools?
Did the virgins have names? Were each of them somehow a re-flection of the inner core, the essential meaning of the virgin and the Kin-dom? I entered into the following dialogue with the images of that parable:

Georgene:
You, O Ten Virgins, just who are you? Do you have
names? What makes some of you wise? Why does the

teller of this tale name some of you as foolish? And just
how is wisdom related to oil for lamps and to being virgin?

The Ten:
We are ten aspects of yourself. The answers to the rest
of your questions will be revealed when you know our
names.

Georgene:
Then, tell me your names.

The Ten:
We are Goodness, Beauty, Truth, Love, and Power. We
are Fear, Compulsion, Domination, Apathy, and
Lechery.

Georgene:
(And all are facets of me? I thought for a long time
before I continued with the conversation.) What is it
that makes you, Goodness, Beauty, Truth, Love, and
Power, wise?

The Wise Virgins:
We are wise because we are rooted in and empowered
by our relationship with the Holy. We see relational
aspects in all of life. For example, when we received
that invitation to the wedding reception, we saw it as a
gathering to celebrate relationship. And we knew that
invitations are related to waiting. Waiting is related to
the movement of the cosmos from light into darkness.
Darkness is related to providing another form of light.
This need is related to lamps and lamps are related to
oil, enough oil until the invitor comes into our waiting.

You see, we know the connections because we are ourselves relating realities. We are wise because we know
that we are, and we are because of our rootedness in the
Holy. I am Goodness and I am enough when I am rooted

in the Good God. I am Beauty and I am enough when I am rooted in the Beautiful God. I am Truth and I am enough when I am rooted in the Truthful God. I am Love and I am enough when I am rooted in Love. I am Power and I am enough when I am rooted in the Powerful God.

Georgene:
And you, Foolish Ones, what is your native essence? What are you like?

The Fools:
We are foolish because we too have the choice to see all of life in relationship, but we renounce this free choice. We only look at ourselves. This is exactly how we fool ourselves. We received the invitation and we only perceived the status of being special guests. We refused to notice that the invitation was related to waiting. All we saw was "I will be honored!" And when the waiting was prolonged into darkness, we were without lamps or oil.

We are not virgins. We have no relational wisdom. We believe that we are the source of our own being. We think that we are enough just because we are. I am Fear! I am Compulsion! I am Domination! I am Apathy! I am Lechery!

Georgene:
What is it about you, you Fools, that keeps you from the revelation and the power of relating wisdom?

The Fools:
Oh, a response to that question is too much like relating or trying to connect things. We don't want to spend the time figuring that out. We'd rather just associate with Virgins and see what we can get through life on their wisdom.

But, as you see in the story, it doesn't really work. Association wasn't enough. We were unaware of the

source of the invitation, and that feast couldn't be experienced through association. Awareness, relational
consciousness, was necessary.

Georgene:
Don't you want to change from being Fools to being
Wise Virgins?

Fools:
Change!? We'd risk our identities!

Georgene:
Yes, I see. The price of wisdom is letting go of imagining
any facet of the self as the source of life. The feast that
is waiting for those who are willing to pay the price is
life as a virgin. And the virgin has the wisdom, the oil, of
relational awareness.

This dialogue continues to be a wisdom webbing for
my life. The fullness of the gift of a virgin cotton ball is
still being revealed. Both the cotton and the dialogue
are re-flections to me of the virgin or of the root source
of my being. And I am becoming even more aware that
all of creation is called to be virgin.

"Wisdom builds her home within you. Wisdom
shines bright and never grows dim. Those who look for
her can easily find her. She is quick to make herself
known to anyone who desires her" (Wisdom 6). I had
read and prayed with this scripture. I had even given
others a retreat on Wisdom's ways.
Then I experienced a series of losses in my life. I
lost a work position. I lost a sense of direction. I lost the
goals and affirmations of that job. I lost an office space.
And all of this felt as if I had lost all and any relationship with Wisdom. I felt devastated. This was a disaster.
I was in a pit. If this was what it felt like to be in relationship with Wisdom, I wanted out. Why hadn't some-

one warned me?

From the mess of these painful losses rose a
memory: I had made a covenant to watch life. And,
here, right before me, was lots of life. And so I began to
watch the darkness, the pain, the devastation, the pit I
seemed to have been put into. I watched all of it as if it
were a mirror that would show me just how all of this
was wisdom's webbings. I watched through my tears
and fears. And I cried and raged with a few companions.

I do not know the exact moment or hour when the
transformation began. But somewhere in the midst of
the watching the pit took on the image of an excavation
dig; a hole indeed, but one in which treasures of the
ages were buried. I discovered a few such treasures of
my life. I washed them with my tears. I held them in my
hopes. I embraced their healing grace with my
gratitude. I came to a new understanding of Wisdom.
All life, even the pits, can be revelations of her love.
The choice to look for her within the pain will always be
mine.

The above stories share some of the connections
that sabbath experiences have issued in my life. Watching life has become the exercise of my spiritual, physical, intellectual, intuitive, and relational life. It is quite
a discipline! Watching life is a constant turning with, an
ever-flowing conversion into the ways of the Kin-dom of
God. Free will continues to be the original, virgin gift
from the Holy. My relational response to this covenant
is my choice to watch life. And so I pray:

God of graciousness, compassion and harmony,
you are our God
we are your people.
Renew us, the face of the earth.

Root us in you,
so that together
we might reveal your graciousness
to all the earth.

Root us in you,
so that together
we might share your compassion
with all the earth.

Root us in you,
so that together
we might issue your harmony
throughout all the earth.

God of all life,
send us your spirit.
Renew your promise
that you are our God
and we are your people,
now and forever.

Amen.

Questions and Suggestions for Re-flection

● During your sabbath spaces and times ask yourself how you would respond to these questions of John's gospel:

> If my relative keeps on sinning against me, how many times do I have to forgive him or her?
> Haven't you read the scriptures that say that in the beginning the Creator made people female and male?
> What do I have to do to receive eternal life?
> Why do you ask me about goodness?
> Are you jealous because I am generous?
> How did the fig tree dry up so quickly?
> Which is more important, the gold or the temple that makes the gold holy?

Which is more important, the gift or the altar
which makes the gift holy?
When did we see you hungry and not feed you?
What do you think?
How is it that you were not able to keep watch
with me?

● During other sabbaths choose an experience of your
life. *Mira.* Watch Life. Record all the questions that the
watching issues. Then write the wisdom story that the
questions reveal.

RE-FLECTION 4

Communions Of The Kin-dom

Let me recall for you some of Morris West's novel *Clowns Of God* (Morrow & Co., 1981). The main character, Jean Marie Barette, at one moment Pope Gregory XVII and at another moment Johnny the Clown, had a revelation about the future of the 20th century. He received a vision that revealed that the only way to transform the political and economic global realities was to embrace the "coming of Christ" as communions of people living in mutuality.

The story explores Barette's attempts to communicate this revelation. It tells us of the varied responses the message and the messenger received. Finally, marginalized by the churches, the governments, and the economic "stewards" of the world's wealth, Johnny the Clown seeks some confirmation of the vision's authenticity. His prayer is answered. A sign is given. A "cosmos cup" and a marginalized woman mirror its revelation.

West's telling of this tale is not unlike John's telling of his vision in the Book of Revelation of the Christian scriptures. In both stories, the message and the mission is communion. And we are told in each of them that if we embrace the message, then we are to expect our lives to be in constant conversion until we are in Kindom communion. I believe both stories mirror Jesus' prayer for the cosmos: "Abba, may they be one in us as you are in me and I am in you." (John 17:21) Communion is the beginning and the end: our God is a communion and the Kin-dom to come is a communion.

Jesus' vision of the Kin-dom was a harmony of the differences in communion. He knew all of creation to be a breathing exchange with the differently enabling life of the creator. The 1st century folk among whom he lived were both attracted and repelled by his vision. But to those who responded, " Where do you and your vision abide?" Jesus invited, "Come and see." And those who followed were called disciples. They were the folk who were willing to watch life through the mirror of communion for the sake of the Kin-dom. They were the folk who were willing to seek the sacred in, through and with communion.

To them Jesus revealed the way: Gather (Mt. 18:20); Be Alert — Mira. (Mt. 25); and then Go, Invite All Into Communion (Lk 10:1). This plan or vision was the way of the God and the kin of the Kin-dom. Communion, companionship, sharing in mutuality was the Kin-dom's beginning and end, and it would be its lure and its fulfillment. Those who followed its way would know the inspiration, the support, the reconciliation, and the challenge of Christ's spirit incarnated in the communions.

We can find images of these communities of formation and conversion in the writings of Peter and Paul and of James and John. The way that some of these communions imaged Christ's message and mission are recorded by Matthew, Mark, Luke, and John, as well as by the not-so-often celebrated gospels of Mary, Philip, and Thomas. Actually, the communion of the Kin-dom is recorded everywhere in the cosmos. Blessed are we who have eyes to see and ears to hear!

The Chinese tell stories of gathering in the realm of a gentle omnipotence, while the Celts imaged the power of communion as magic, enchantment, and divination. The Americas' Indians gathered, and continue to do so, with a spirit of oneness that is the foundation of all

dualities as they breathe mutuality. The Semitic
peoples lived with an imagination of the goddesses and
gods who led them by the hand from chaos into harmony. Some of the ancients of Africa have been gathering in the name of the Divine Ancestress of all peoples.
Many Islanders have lived with an image of the sacred
not unlike a mother bird who hovers, watching and car-
ing for all of life. Actually, virgin peoples of all places
have always gathered and breathed with the elements
of the cosmos: fire, air, water, earth, space, and depth.
In union with the Lunar Trinity and her re-flecting companions, creatures have come to know and be known in
communions of the Kin-dom.

   We who name ourselves Christian can trace our
history of gathering back to Jesus and his spirit. Our
forms of communion are named and mirrored in patterns not unlike that of a multi-faceted webbing. Each
facet is the result of a connecting of different environments, needs, and gifts. We have not always embraced
those differences with harmony. We continue to struggle for full communion. Yet Christ's spirit has continually invited all sacred-searching peoples to re-flect, renew, and remember the God of the Kin-dom: a God of
graciousness, compassion, and harmony.

   Some of our Christian communities have been and
continue to be revelations of the service of spiritual and
corporal works of mercy. Others are organizations
orientated toward worship, word, ritual, and/or human
growth. It is the needs of the universe that the spirit
uses to lure peoples into communion. There is a fluidity
both about the kinds of gatherings and about the life of
the communities. Somehow, this seems right to me. The
communions ought to re-flect the fluidity of the God
named Yahweh, an ever-flowing I AM WHO I AM
WHO I AM WHO...

   Yet, for most of us, our need for security issues
many questions about communities: Do groups, as do individuals, have personalities? Do they have develop-
mental and dying patterns? Do we need different ways

of gathering at different times of our lives? Who provides for our need for communion? Who gathers a community? Why do we feel guilty when we need to change
our communion relationship? Have we been grasped by
the myth that says that systems, especially Christian
communities, ought to live forever in exactly the same
way as we think that they began? How will we pass on
the message and mission of the Christian communion to
our young?

There are more questions. But for the purpose of
this Re-flection, the ones named are sufficient to highlight our dilemma. Here I will address one of the questions: Do communities have stages of beginning,
developing, and dying? My experiences and re-flections
respond in the affirmative.

First, there is an identity process. Through this
stage the members of the community name their needs
and the gifts that they bring into the communion. This
could be called a creedal stage. The process can take a
long time. Sometimes it is a joyful experience and sometimes it is a painful experience. Learning how to graciously and compassionately accept others' differences
is indeed a preciously tender process. The myth that
uniformity is the desired image for the community does
not die easily. But it must die if the communion is to re-
flect the God of the Kin-dom. Along with it we must
bury all comparisons of each other to one another or of
the community to another community. It is through the
identity process that each member comes to know her
or his virgin gifts. And it is through this very process
that a communion of the gifts of the spirit is formed.

The communion that knows itself as a re-flection of
the God of the Kin-dom grows naturally into the next
process: the intimacy stage of development. The community must ask, "How will we continue to be honest
with each other when we are in constant conversion
ourselves?" Rituals need to be developed during this
process that will both celebrate and reconcile the community members as each tries to faithfully live the iden-

tity of the communion. That which will not be named, that which we hide from each other, that very facet will eventually destroy the communion.

Another process that all communions experience is the struggle to be generative. We know from a long reflective history that the gifts of the spirit are always given to individuals. Usually these individuals are members of a communion. But the gifts are never given for the sake of the individual. They are always for the sake of the community. Thus, the individual's gifts are for sharing within the community and beyond the community. A community aware of its gifts and acknowledging the source of the gifts must be of service, be it the service of bread sharing or the service of foot washing. Both are eucharist for the Christian communion.

Another issue that most communions are encountering today is the facet of the differently abled sexualities of their members. Whenever we gather we come as bodies; flesh and blood beings who are habits or vestments or sacred masks for our spirits, emotions, thoughts, and intuitions. Our sexuality, how we are as females and how we are as males, will effect the communion. To deny or exclude these differing gifts will limit the communion's revelation of the Kin-dom. Our sexuality must be identified, acknowledged, blessed, and celebrated by the community if it wants to continue to identify itself as a Christian communion.

When we accept the invitation to Kin-dom communion, we accept these processes and ways of the Kin-dom. Change, conversion, is one of the hallmarks of the Kin-dom. Thus we must be committed to conversion. Commitment is not so much a matter of time, whether we name it as temporary or permanent, as it is a matter of willingness to work for the revelation of the Kin-dom. Work is not a word we frequently associate with community. But that is an error. Discernment of the spirit's presence and gifts, of my and others' needs, of how to be of service, is hard work. It takes much energy. The cost is consciousness that does not sleep. There are no short-range plans for the formation of Christian communions. And Kin-dom time can only be told in relationship to the shared gifts of joy, peace, patience, fortitude, courage, wonder, beauty, truth, and goodness.

Christ's spirit invites and empowers us to re-flect the message and mission of the Kin-dom. We are called to Gather, to Be Alert, and to Go Among All. We can be transformed into such disciples through communities who embrace both the ecstatic and the prophetic energies of the spirit. The choice remains ours. Will we respond to the invitation as communions of the Kindom?

Questions and Suggestions for Re-flection

● What communion experiences have nourished you in the past?

● What communions lure you today?

● How is this communion, or are these communions serving the kin of the Kin-dom?

● What gifts do you bring to the communion?

● What needs do you share with the community?

● As you ponder your Christian community experiences, what questions come to your mind?

● How do you share the gift of your sexuality within and beyond the community?

● How does the community name, bless, celebrate, and share the differing gifts of sexuality of its members?

● Wonder with these questions from Matthew's gospel:

Do you want us to go and pull up the weeds?
Do you understand these things about the Kin-dom?
Where will we find enough food to feed this crowd?
How much bread do you have?
Don't you remember when I broke the bread
for five thousand?
Will you gain anything if you win the whole
world but lose your life?

RE-FLECTION 5

 Imaging The Sacred

Like all children, we get enraptured with mystery. Even the "Remember when..." game can intrigue us for hours. And somewhere in the midst of the intrigue, we are touched by the Sacred/Creating/Relating mystery. The pattern keeps repeating itself: Life reveals the sacred and the sacred re-flects more life. It is almost like playing on a merry-go-round. Thus was the lure, I believe, in Jesus' call: Remember, the Kin-dom of God belongs to the child. (Luke 18:12) The Kin-dom is of and for those who will play. It is incarnated in, through, and with those who will question and who will take the time to remember life's mysterious and intriguing experiences. These children know that through such living the sacred is continually imaged.

Can you recall your first memory of God? Do you remember when it was that the concept "God" moved within you into being an alive relationship? When you were instructed through your faith communions that you were created in the image and likeness of God, what images of the sacred appeared in your awareness?

Through such questions and re-flections our personal theologies make themselves conscious. Each of us has a personal, historical, environmental theology. The resources of these theologies are rooted in our experiences of family, nature, education, community, art, scripture, friendships, hardships, celebrations, the body, the mind, prayer, etc. Each encounter with life reveals another facet of the ever-forming image of the ever-flowing sacred.

In order to share our theologies we need to tell stories. Stories help us notice the patterns or webbings of our relationship with the sacred. They stretch the tellers of the tales as well as the listeners. It is as if stories are the kneading of the bread of life. Each story lures us to re-flect and question our life. The questions draw us to look at our values, to choose new values, or to renew those we treasure. The new or renewed values become as mirrors where we can see our behaviors. These behaviors are the "stuff" of life around which we tell stories. And so the webbing of wisdom continues.

Here are some stories that sacred-searching folk have shared with me. *Mira!* Watch and remember. Let each story re-flect new questions to you. Let your child play with the responses as she or he images the sacred. Ask, along with the tellers of these tales: What is my image of the sacred like? How does this image effect and affect my daily lived experiences?

Irene didn't know how to put a name on her renewed relationship with her God, but she could tell the story of when it became known to her and what it looked like:

Recently she had an appointment with her doctor. When she entered the waiting room of the doctor's office, she was overwhelmed by the number of people occupying it. The room was filled! As she looked around for a seat, she noticed that a good number of the patients were retarded children. The rest of the folk had their heads buried in magazines. She felt awkward in the presence of these differently abled children. But she knew she couldn't hide. She took a seat next to a child who rocked back and forth while mumbling into space. She sensed a oneness with him as she sat and listened to the babbling. This was a new behavior for her. She knew that this child, too, was loved by the sacred. And she knew that she was re-flecting such love, the same love she had received; the love of just being present.

Once, I felt that my relationship with the sacred was like riding a roller coaster. Yes, a roller coaster! The anticipation, the fear, the excitement, and the lures of God were all mixed into one emotion that was almost unnameable, just like all was mixed up when I rode a roller coaster. Both issued a sense of loss of my control. Yet both also issued a new sense of freedom. Both stretched me in many ways. Both brought refreshment. Both made me feel like I wanted to scream: "My God!" and shout a need that only silence could express. Through both I became breathlessly grateful for life.

John said that at one time he was out in "left field" with his relationship with God. But lately, probably because of the kind of people at the church where he was involved, he felt that he was playing on the same team as God. And he was doing pretty well! He was on second base and running. He knew that there was more to come because he longed for home plate.

Mary said that she remembered a time in her life when she was going through many changes. She felt lost, abandoned, frustrated, trapped, confused, and unwanted. Most of these feelings got acted out with her family and that hadn't helped matters at all.

Then one day she found herself daydreaming. She sensed herself falling out of a boat into deep water. She fought the water. But it was a losing struggle. She was drowning. Then something happened. She relaxed. She realized that she was swimming and that with this power she could make some choices. She could swim to the shore. She could get back into the boat. Or she could play in the water.

This daydream made her question her daily living and her relationship with God. She began to image both life and God as the water. She could continue to fight the water or choose to be at home with it. She had a choice. If she exercised it, she would not drown. And it was even OK to get back into the boat.

Now she was enjoying her family in a new way. And they were glad she was "at home."

These stories and all of our stories help us to reflect on our images of the sacred. The sacred is always issuing the power for us to do so, for such is the nature of graciousness. Graciousness is an image of the sacred that is pregnant with generosity. It is an image that will help us to embrace life with the full knowledge of the proximate trouble that gracious living will meet in this competitive world. It is a power, a grace, that lures us into our virgin being.

This image of the sacred gives birth to a spirit of life that celebrates. When we celebrate we embrace life, knowing that no part of life can be more powerful than the source of life itself: the sacred. Our image of the sacred is always the foundation of our spirituality. Our spirituality is the breath of our behaviors. And our behaviors re-flect our image of the sacred.

Questions and Suggestions for Re-flection

● Can you name some of your images of God with four or five different adjectives, verbs, or analogies?

● Remember a personal story of encountering the sacred:

What happened?
How did you feel?
What did you think?
What did it reveal to you about life?

● Share your individual response to the above re-flection with your faith-sharing community.

● When your community gathers next time, take a sab-bath to re-flect and share upon these questions:

> What is the image of the God that we worship?
> How do we celebrate, or do we celebrate out of, this image?

RE-FLECTION 6

 Our Vision Of Prayer

Our vision of prayer is rooted in our vision of the sacred. Therefore, the question that issues from our image of prayer is: How do we respond to life out of our relationship with the sacred?

All of us have been taught and have practiced a variety of prayers. For most of us, these prayers have been developed in response to an image of the holy that is outside of our ordinary, daily experiences. Thus our prayers have been means to make ourselves come closer to God or to make the distant God come closer to us. We have accepted a definition of prayer as the lifting up of our minds and hearts to this transcendant sacredness.

This definition of prayer is only expressive of a partial vision. It does not invite our total created human nature to respond to God. For example, the senses are not included. And if "our minds" means our intellects and "our hearts" means our wills, as patriarchal theologians would have us believe, then only those "worthy" parts pray. We need a vision of prayer that includes our whole body along with our values, emotions, intuitions, and relationships because all are able to respond to the sacred mystery.

And what if the sacred source of all life is already present? Does that mean that there is no one to "lift up" to and therefore no need to pray? What if our image of God is that of both an intimate presence and a transcending, transforming power? How do we then define prayer? Or, perhaps prayer is an experience that cannot be defined. Perhaps prayer is that which can only be described by those who participate in the experience! How can we describe a mutual exchange of breath, or a mystery-centered vision of prayer that includes our lived experiences of both the presence and the absence of the sacred?

For me (and each of us must learn to describe our own experience), prayer is like being rooted in God like a tree of life. It is also like breathing with the holy. And it is like crying out, "Hallowed be thy name!" and knowing the response as an echo in a hollow space at my center, "Be thy name, Georgene!" Sometimes, prayer appears to be a pulsating process of giving and receiving. At other times, it is like being embraced and choosing to embrace, even the lepers of life. Always, prayer is a response to an awareness of the energy of graciousness.

Prayer, then, can be described as a radical response to life. Radical means rooted, as a radish is a root. Radical means grounded, as when one is planted in a source of life. The sacred mystery whom we seek is the ground of all creation. We are rooted in this goodness, truth, and beauty. When we choose to respond to, and with, and from, and through all of our lived experiences from such rootedness, we are praying.

We have, as individuals and as a people, experienced many ways of rooting ourselves in the sacred. Some of these ways have been comfortable. Some have been challenging. Some prayer ways have named and deplored the attitudes of us humans and thus challenged us to embrace the uprooting that is needed. We have experienced rituals, rote prayers, chants, dialogical prayers, and many other forms of personal and communal prayer. For some of us, these kinds of prayer have been natural; for others of us, they are unnatural. They may be responses to life for some, but not always for all.

Our image or vision of the sacred changes as we live alert lives. So, too, must our responses to life

change. Thus, our prayer is always changing. We need
to live with the questions: What way of response does
my image of the sacred call me to today? Or at this time
of my life? Or at this time of the community's life? How
do I describe myself as a woman or man of prayer? How
would I describe my response to the life I am rooted in?
What life do I encounter that needs to be uprooted?

The following are some possible descriptions of
prayer:

Natural Ecstasy:
When I ask people to explain the experiences of
God that they have had and how they remember responding because of them, they inevitably tell me
stories. The following are some examples of their
descriptions of prayer.

*I ran three miles today. It seemed like I lost
myself. When I was finished I felt connected with
everyone and everything. My God, I was alive!*

●

*I was walking in the woods. I was trying to get
some space from all that I had to do. Yet, it seemed
that the work was all that I could think about.
When I returned to my parked car, I realized that
I'd been walking for two hours. But it had only
seemed like ten minutes.*

●

*Our family prepared and delivered a meal to a
sick neighbor. It was strange, be we felt like we
were the ones who were fed and healed.*

●

*I know heaven. It is when I'm making love
with Al.*

●

*I remember several wonderful things that our
family did together. We went to church. We visited
family and friends on Sundays and holidays. We
went for rides to "see the lake" and to "get lost" in*

*the country. We went fishing. Somehow all of
these times together gave me the same holy feelings.*

In all of these stories, these sabbath expressions,
there are some common facets. There is choice. There is
the sense of losing oneself. There is some element of
surprise. Time is experienced differently. And each
issues a natural refreshment. These descriptions of
prayer, of awareness of the sacred and of a response to
it, can be called prayers of natural ecstasies.

Prayer really can be that natural and that ecstatic!

Re-flection:

The awareness of response that enables us to identify experiences as prayer is the power or grace of re-
flection. Re-flection is a way of looking at life as we look
into a mirror. The mirror gives back what we put in. The
mirror can show us our inner life. We need to develop
skills and resources that will make us more alert to our
inner life as it breathes with our outer life. Together,
they are our spiritual life. The inner life is the place
where we understand how it is and in whom it is that we
are rooted.

Re-flection leads us to let go of our false images of
the sacred, of creation and of ourselves. Re-flection
lures us into new images of life and the mysteries of the
holy. Re-flection helps us to know and accept ourselves
as limited creatures who are playing, wondering, and
working with the unlimited richness of the Gracious
God.

Re-flection is the inner core, the wisdom of all
meditation methods. It takes time and it requires space.
Sabbath is the scriptural language of re-flection space
and time. Have we lost the sabbath sense? Have we
abandoned re-flection as prayer? Is that why we do not
know how to make connections and to see ourselves in
mutual relationship with all the kin of the earth?

Telling Our Life Story:

Questions about our relationship with the sacred guide us through a spiritually alert course to another experience of prayer: our life story. Each one of us is a reflection of the fullness of life and of the sacred. To know this fullness and to know its source, its rooting ground, we need to be able to recognize and embrace our unique life experience. Not to accept our life story is to choose some form of suicide. We need to remember and reroot in order to see the webbings. When the connections are a part of our awareness, our past and present and future gather as the revelation of life. Then we have a story to tell.

Telling our life story is an expression of prayer. We can learn how and when to pray this way. There are many tools available: books, tapes, videos and workshops. Perhaps no tool is as powerful as is the process of journaling. It is a way to record our awarenesses and to hold them until the wisdom of the webbings can be known. A journal, used regularly, can become the personal scriptures, the stories of our creation, salvation, and ministry.

Expression And Silence:

No matter how we choose to radically respond to life, we engage in the paradox of expression and silence. As we become more aware of our rootedness in God, we choose some balance between these two dynamics. The balance is necessary in order to reveal and to reverence our experiences, our prayer. But sometimes the experience of this balancing feels like what we call "falling in love." We want the world to know, yet we want to keep "our secret" hidden from everyone. Or our prayer can resemble our experiences at symphonies, movies, or with a good book. We know that no one else could possibly experience what we have, yet, we want everyone to have the experience. We want to cherish our truth as special, yet we want to share it with all. Such are the dynamics of expression and silence at play within our prayer.

Silence is the home of expression when it issues strength and nourishment to our words and gestures. Words and gestures can reveal the mystery that we encountered in the silence. Both can be shared with companions. And together, both expression and silence issue harmony to share with the earth.

The Environment Of Prayer:

Where do we pray? This Re-flection has tried to respond to this question through the many facets of prayer that it has explored. The root response is that we pray in, through and with life. We need, therefore, to become aware of the environments of our lives.

Awareness, or attention itself, is an environment of prayer. When and where are we most aware? In quiet spaces? In busy parks? At home? In a sacred place? In the midst of a party? In the midst of deafening solitude? When surrounded by beauty? Or when naked poverty shows her face? Only we can know what will fulfill the environmental needs that will best empower us to be rooted and responsive to life. Again, the choice is ours.

Whatever expression or experience we choose in order to radically respond to life, and whenever we choose with awareness and/or with enthusiasm (in the spirit), we are praying. When we re-flect on the natural ecstasies of our life stories, we pray. When we tell the stories, we pray. When we midwife more life with each other, we pray. When we let the words and the gestures and the silences generate new possibilities for the revelation of the holy, we pray. And whenever we share life out of our Kin-dom alertness, we are women and men of prayer. Such a vision of our prayer will issue a global consciousness that breathes with all creation. Such a vision of prayer will provide a multitude of sabbath bread.

Questions and Suggestions for Re-flection

● Recall the description of prayer that you were given as a child. How did you pray then? How do you pray now? How would you describe prayer to a child today?

● What body movements, actions, gestures, thoughts, practices, corporal works of mercy, and spaces of solitude and silence do you weave into your prayer?

● Re-flect on the prayer styles of your community. Do you practice a variety of prayer styles in order to include all the different needs of the community members? Has anyone in the community ever asked you how you would like to pray? How can the individuals' needs be incorporated into the public prayer of the community?

● When was the last time that your communion took the time to listen to the life stories of its members?

● What kind of relationships would develop among a kin who knew each others' stories?

● What care do you take to create your prayer environment?

● How can you become more aware of your rootedness in and responsiveness to and with the sacred?

RE-FLECTION 7

 Incarnation

What comes to your mind when you read the mystery of the incarnation? Here are some of my associations:

a baby
God becomes human
an angel with a message
a birth in Bethlehem
a woman's "Yes"
a breakthrough
affirmation
sacred word and breath in human flesh
a new covenant
people of the Kin-dom
a sign for the times
stars
searchers
"The word became flesh and made a tent among us."
"Know that the Kin-dom is within you."
"Who is my mother, my brother or my sister?"
"Live in me as I live in you."
How close is the divine presence?
What am I supposed to do now?

Like all mysteries, the incarnation can only be known or seen in parts or facets. This Re-flection is a series of story-facets and some re-flections. Each one invites you: *mira!*

A Story From Santarem, Brazil

Not so long ago, I received a letter from John, a Franciscan missionary ministering among the Amazon peoples. He wanted to share with me the spirit of the people of a barrio and their Christmas ritual.

John wrote: "We gathered outside the hut of a woman who is very active in the mothers club and is a prostitute. She had been sick during most of the year. But this is where the community leaders wanted to celebrate because they believe that Christ is most revealed by the poorest. At the offering in the ritual the people gave the woman some food. And all during our celebration we had a live nativity scene. It was an unwed mother and her baby."

John concluded his letter to me by saying that, "When you leave the story of Jesus to the poor people to tell, they tell it with their lives. That is really all that they have. It has to be enough."

Re-flection:

Isn't our life always enough? That was and is the good news of the incarnation. God spoke the language that women and men comprehended: their own human flesh, blood, and spirit. Jesus was enough. He would re-teach us that we are enough. If only we could now learn this language well enough for it to become the mother tongue of all the kin of the earth!

A Story From Calcutta, India

The gentle man, Dan, who related this experience to me was making a journey/retreat, a pilgrimage, among several lands of the Far East. He was seeking a deeper understanding of the mystery of the sacred, as others have come to know it. However, as he traveled he began to sense an absence of something of his own Christian faith. But just what it was he couldn't say. It was in the city of Calcutta that the absence incarnated in his being.

Dan had walked in the early morning, along with

the monk who was to teach him meditation, through the poverty, death, and human pain of the city. When they arrived at the temple, he was instructed to empty his mind and to spend the time in meditation. From what he could observe, his teacher was doing just that. But Dan could not rid his mind, his heart, nor his senses of the people that he had encountered on the journey to the temple. Later that evening, they reversed the journey and arrived at their hut. The time here was to be spent nourishing the body and in rest. But, again, Dan could do neither with any peace. So he broke the silence of the night and asked the monk for instruction on ridding himself of the images of the peoples that they had walked among that day.

The monk replied, "Pay attention to your own karma. Don't get involved in others' karma."

That was the breakthrough moment of insight for Dan. He was a Christian. And the God of the Christian faith had gotten involved in others' lives, so involved that the divine took the flesh of the people. He must reject the monk's teaching.

Once this journey from the experience of absence to questioning, and from re-flection to insight had been traveled, Dan could no longer stay with the monk. He went to find a new teacher who could help him get involved in the lives and deaths of the people he had walked among. The mystery of the incarnation could not remain just an insight for him. He had to act it out with his own flesh, blood, and spirit.

Re-flection:

If our God embraced our human life in the fullest possible way, by becoming human, how then are we to embrace human life? When the sacred breaks through into our lives, are we not to share that power among our kin? It seems to me that this is the faith foundation of the issues of our day: peace, justice, and human rights.

Justice means the right ordering of life. If the divine order for life is to get involved, can we, as believers in

the incarnation, do anything less and still remain just?
Jesus said, "The Kin-dom of God is within you." He
literally knew that. And he didn't exclude anyone. Are
we, as Christians, not then committed to be our sisters'
and brothers' keepers? As Marjorie Tuite declared with
her life: We must think globally and then we must act
locally.

A Story From Mid-America, U.S.A.

Terry was participating in a spiritual renewal process with a faith community. The people of that communion were to spend some time each day re-flecting
on the faith mystery that the group had explored at their
weekly gathering. Terry chose to spend his time while
he made his daily journey to his job. He had to take a
train from his suburban home to his central city work.
On one particular day Terry was re-flecting with: "And
the word became flesh and dwelt among us."

As he pondered the meaning of this for his life, his
eyes wandered with the many differently enriched and
impoverished neighborhoods through which the train
traveled. His mind began to explore the school busing
issue. He had always felt quite safe from having to
make any decisions about this issue for his children because inter-municipal busing law wasn't in practice. But
he had read that a case on this issue was pending in a
federal court. What would he do if that became a law of
the land?

Somewhere in the midst of that question, Terry remembered that he was supposed to be re-flecting on the
mystery of the incarnation. So he refocused his eyes
and his mind on: "And the word became flesh and
dwelt among us." What did that mean for him now? As
the neighborhoods continued to flash by the train win-
dows, his thoughts flashed back to the busing issue.
Then he caught himself again and returned to is original
intended focus.

Terry told the group at their next gathering, "I don't
remember how many times that rhythm was repeated.

But at one of the readings of the scriptures the thought occurred to me: What a busing job the incarnation was! The divine had to travel from the Kin-dom to earth and into a woman's body and then be born among us, mere humans. Well, I still haven't settled the busing issue in my own heart, but I certainly understand the trust and affirmation of the incarnation more deeply."

Re-flection:
The incarnation is trust at its sacred best! Do we treasure that which has been so entrusted to us? How do we steward the gift? What does stewardship for and because of the mystery of incarnation look like today for those of us who know that the dwelling of the sacred among us is not just a thing of the past?

A Story From Nazareth, Israel
Not so long ago, as sacred time is measured, mystery broke into the life of a woman and asked her to choose a radical stewardship. Would she receive the sacred in a way that only the sacred could make possible? Was she willing to accept a Kin-dom possibility in the midst of her earthly living? Would she allow the divine to become so involved in her life that the child she would issue in birth would be the full revelation of the Kin-dom?

Well, that was quite a request! And like any of us, Mary had a few questions of her own: "Who, me? Just how will this involvement take place, and how long will it last? What will this mean for the rest of my life?"

All of her wonderings were not fully answered. But she was assured that she would be enough, just as she was! And, with that bit of comfort, she accepted a stewardship for full relationship with sacred possibilities. Thus, a woman began to tell the story of divine imagination with her very own body. Her body was where mystery had emptied itself into an embryo.

Re-flection:

Graciousness in abundance had inhabited Mary's limited imagination. We call this incarnation. And creation has never been the same! We know the rest of the story: Mary issued a son and named him Jesus. He embraced human life in the fullest possibility. He lived, died, rose, and issued the spirit which continues to breathe abundant possibilities of graciousness among all the kin of the Kin-dom.

Mary, since her acceptance of stewardship for incarnation, has been the most abled among all humans to proclaim: "This is my body. This is my blood." We who name ourselves disciples of the message and mission of her son, Jesus the Christ, are the stewards of the same mystery of incarnation. And we, by our choice of the Christian faith, are ordained to continue the proclamation of the divine among all the kin: "You are my body. You are my blood."

Questions and Suggestions for Re-flection

● What was the meaning of incarnation for you at the age of ten? at the age of 25? today?

● What values or feelings are touched within yourself when you hear words like "get involved" or "stewardship"?

● Take a sabbath with the words: "And the word became flesh and dwelt among us." What does this mean for your daily living?

● Spend a sabbath with your community exercising the affirmation of the incarnation in this way:

> In silence, let each member of the gathering consider every other member and record an affirmation of each one. Then, end the silence and let one person receive the affirmations of their goodness from everyone else. After a person has re-

ceived all of the group's gifts, she or he might take a
moment to just treasure what this incarnation
power feels like. Then another person chooses to
receive the affirmations of the group.

● For what justice are you responsible?

● How is your community a responsible steward of
justice among the kin?

● What is our right to life?

RE-FLECTION 8

 Jesus

Jesus looked at Peter and said, "Who do you say that I am?" (Matt. 16:15)

The journey in Christian faith is a process of responding to this question. And in the midst of the experience, we encounter both our extreme poverty and our abundant richness. We search and cry out for identification, for affirmation, and for direction. We wonder if our life experiences are to be trusted. Can they reveal the divine imagination? Are they a religious experience or a grand self-deception? What will we do when we encounter evil? To whom can we turn to for companionship? Has anyone ever so journeyed and remained faithful?

We look for maps, for images, for visions that will direct our journey. We search for order, for affirmation, and for a call. We desire companions. We seek revelations of truth in our questions, in our churches, in our books, creeds, rituals, signs, and symbolic and mythical persons. Finally, as Christians, we find consolation in a name that Jesus claimed: "I am the way, the truth, and the life." (Jn. 14:6)

But who is this Jesus for us today? How does the way, the truth, and the life that he is evolve in our daily lives? The image or vision of Jesus Christ in which we orientate ourselves will issue our behaviors, for our actions are the re-flections of our imaginations. So we look again and ask more questions.

Traditions are an important element in our imaginations. Yet we know that our vision of Jesus will have little effect in our daily living if we root it only in traditions. We have to critique the tradition. We have to critique the tellers of those tales, and we have to critique our personal experiences. We have to critique them in the light of our community's vision, for it is in community that we come to trust the spirit's power and its revelation of the way, the truth, and the life.

An image of Jesus that is rooted in the Christian community is that of him as the namer of the indiscriminately gracious sacred. Jesus, the community has come to believe, was sent with this message and mission. Naming was his ministry. He struggled as he came to know his mission. Then he embraced it with conviction. It was at the beginning of his public life, as professed by the community gathered with Luke, that Jesus proclaimed that he was indeed the namer:

> "The spirit of God is upon me: I have been anointed. I have been sent to bring glad tidings to the poor, to proclaim liberty to captives, recovery of sight to the blind, and release to prisoners: to announce, to name, the Kindom of God." (Lk. 4:18-19)

The community records that after Jesus had witnessed that he himself was the namer of the possibilities for a new harmony, he then lived the truth of this mission. At the end he was questioned by Pilot. He then declared:

> "The reason I was born, the reason I came into the world is to name the truth." (Jn. 18:37)

And the community who had gathered with Matthew remembered Jesus' final proclamation when he passed on his mission and his power to name:

> "Go, therefore, and make disciples of all nations. Baptize them in the name of the of the Kin-dom's God." (Mt. 28:19)

Jesus was and is the namer of the sacred. As he inhabited this truth, he released the power of our original created truth, thus enabling us to name ourselves as daughters and sons of the sacred. Through this same life, he also released our power to ward off all that could destroy, hinder, separate, or annihilate the full revelation of life. Jesus revealed the experience, the direction, the order, the affirmation, and the call; all was now possible through faithful living with the mystery of the indiscriminately gracious sacred.

After his ascension, Jesus' disciples were further empowered to continue the proclamation of the message and mission of the namer. And, today, we Christians are that same empowered possibility. We are the namer. This is our gift. This is our message. Naming is our mission. Naming is our ministry.

Ministry is a term that we used to use when we wanted to describe the work of the ordained or designated leaders of a community. However, today we use it to name what all of us are about when we empower each other to know, claim, and proclaim our true identity as receivers and revealers of the sacred. All creatures really minister to all other creatures. This is the nature of our virgin beings. Today, we are becoming conscious that ministry is reality that re-flects the truth that the word symbolizes.

In this light, we can say that Jesus' entire existence is identical with ministry. He literally spent his life empowering others to name, claim, and proclaim the revelation of their worth, their truth. Jesus, in and through and with his ministry, issued such harmony! He had come from the harmony of the indiscriminately gracious sacred. He saw himself as the namer of the possibilities for such harmony to again fully breathe among us. And he has missioned us to minister the same possibilities.

Another image of Jesus is that of a "midwife." A midwife is a namer in action who trusts the freedom of

those she or he is companioning as they name new life.
The midwife needs to know the past, the history of those
who have conceived the child. The midwife webs that
knowledge, along with knowledge of the birthing process, together with alert attention to the present. Each
moment is new and it is now. However, the energy, the
power that is needed to web the past and the present into "now" is funded from the future—a hope for more
life. When hope collapses into the separate revelations
of woman and child, the midwife's ministry is often
completed. The nourishment and the formation of the
new life together with the healing and celebration of
the woman becomes the service that the community
must provide.

The ministerial style of the historical Jesus re-
sembles midwifery. Jesus was ever aware of the kin in
relationship with the sacred. He was aware of both
their life force and of their death-dealing power. He
webbed his relationship with ancestors, along with the
folk among whom he lived, together with the reality of
Roman occupation. He acted in the midst of this webbing with full attention to the present and to the yet-
to-be revealed life of the Kin-dom. The future, the hope,
the possibilities of Kin-dom motivated all his teaching,
his healing, and his meal ministry. Once his presence
witnessed to and enabled a new revelation of the Kin-
dom's power, Jesus left. The community had to nourish,
invite, form, and mission the new life that had been issued through his companionship.

Midwifery is a learned and gifted ministry. It is a
service funded by a hope in the future and webbed with
the past and present. The midwife is self-giving, paying
attention to others' needs. He or she will not be of service if his or her own needs are projected onto those
being companioned. The midwife's needs are not
denied, but are ministered to at another time and in
another place. That is part of the discipline that the
midwife embraces when this service is chosen as her or
his way of ministering in the community.

If Jesus' ministerial style was that of midwifery, what ought we to be re-flecting through the Christian community's ministry? Is our thinking, our imaging, our action webbing an awareness of the past, along with attention to the present, together with a hope in the future provided by Kin-dom power? Are our services companioning the possibilities for new life? Do we organize our ministries so that they serve the needs of the midwives as well as the needs of those who need such service?

Jesus' naming mission was a midwifing service. He believed in the possibility of the love and power of the Kin-dom to come to new life among us. We name ourselves Christians, disciples of Jesus the Christ. Do our services among the kin of the earth re-present the naming mission that he embraced? Do our services, as the Christian community, continue the revelation of the indiscriminately gracious sacred?

Questions and Suggestions for Re-flection

● Complete this re-flection statement in ten different ways:
    Because Jesus_____, I (we)_____.

● What other images of Jesus do you see re-flected in the scriptures?

● Spend a sabbath with the healing ministry of Jesus. Spend a sabbath with the preaching ministry of Jesus. How did he name the possibilities for harmony through these ministries?

● How is your ministry a naming of the Kin-dom possibilities?

● Is your ministry rooted in hope for the Kin-dom yet to come? Or are you overwhelmed with the present needs?

● How do you need to be served by the community?

● How can your service midwife more hope in new life?

● What are you called to name and midwife for the sake of the Kin-dom?

● How does your service among the kin reveal the indiscriminate graciousness of the sacred power of the Kin-dom?

● Re-flect on all the above question in relationship to your community.

RE-FLECTION 9

The Paschal Event

This Re-flection is an exploration of three experiences in the life of Jesus. They occurred during the
days that he ate his last meal with friends, was arrested,
condemned and crucified, and was resurrected as the
Christ. To see these experiences as the webbings of a
mysterious event, it is necessary to look at each experience from differing stances. Here are three mirrors
for your re-flective stances with the paschal event.
Mira!

A Mirror For Observing A Meal

A meal is an experience of both communion and
solitude through which our whole person is nourished:
mind, heart, body, and spirit. We are fed with memory
as well as with hope. Even though we individually eat
the food, the food we ingest symbolizes communal relationships. When we participate in a meal, we share with
all of creation as it makes possible the act of eating. And
we can say that when we consume this life, we nourish
the whole of creation. From this stance we can see that a
meal is a natural sacrament; an outward sign that continues to issue the life of the sacred.

Now, when the subject is Jesus and a meal is men-
tioned, we immediately think of his Last Supper. We do
this because of the proximity of that meal with Jesus'
death. It is a natural connection, for whenever we lose
anyone we love, we mourn and grieve. We tell stories
about the last "ordinary" experiences that we shared

with that person. Sometimes we even embellish the
stories in order to impress our memories and to affec-
tively effect the listener's imagination. We cherish our
memories by reenacting the last moments we had with
the one we now desire to be with. We hope that through
the stories and the actions, through our memories and
desires, we will know her or his presence again.

This was the very reaction of the first post-death
followers of Jesus. It was the same reaction of the post-
ascension Christians. Those folk gathered to remember
Jesus. They yearned to make the absent Jesus present.
They told stories about him. They ritualized their last
meal with him. They gathered as kin in their domains
and broke the bread of their memories, hopes, and
tables. And they were not sent away hungry. The presence of he who had revealed the Kin-dom among them,
Jesus the Christ, was with them.

Thus, participating in a meal was the beginning of
Eucharistic liturgy. This liturgical form has had many
differing shapes over the centuries. In some sense, the
form has moved from a meal to a drama. Now many
communions are reclaiming the meal ritual. But basical-
ly, our memorial ritual is this webbing of the communion and the solitude of a remembering people who
are gathered to make the absent Jesus present.

The Last Supper was only one of many meals that
Jesus shared with others. When he preached, he often
used the meal as a symbol of the Kin-dom of God. His
healing and naming of the possibilities of harmony was
usually within the context of the sharing of food. Jesus'
disciples have recorded an amazing number of meals in
the gospel stories. It is those stories that makes one wonder: What did Jesus understand about the mystery of a
meal? Why did he use it as the sign of the real presence
of the sacred? Did he want to reveal that the need for
nourishment is common to all kin, regardless of race,
creed, age, culture, sex, economic, or political status?
Did he intend to boldly proclaim that the fullness of a
feast is a sign of the indiscriminately gracious sacred?

Was he ordaining, once and for all, the truth that "meal ministry" and the "service of feet washing" is the way to share the love and power of God with the kin? Are we all expected to be such ministers through our baptism as kin of the Kin-dom? Was Jesus telling us that the setting of the meal was not as important as what happened among the women and men when they shared a common life, a common hunger for bread and drink, and remembered their common roots in the sacred?

Jesus named all of these *mira* possibilities. One of the truths of the "multiplication" stories of the gospel is that there will always be enough food among people who are willing to share in the indiscriminately gracious life of God. As a matter of fact, there will be leftovers because our needs cannot exhaust the gifts of the sacred source of life. Sharing can teach us that there is no need to grasp, to clutch or to cling to riches. If we do grasp, all we have is what we hold now. But if we will share, there will be more from where that was issued: the embrace of graciousness, our God. Through meals Jesus taught that the "poor" share and the "rich" accumulate. Blessed are the poor!

Meal, then, is a natural sacrament of graciousness. It is a ritual of mystery, of nourishment, of companionship, and of the presence of the Kin-dom. It symbolizes what it effects: more life. At his last meal before his death, Jesus asked his companions, "Remember me?" Yes, it was a question. And it is the question addressed to us today: "Will you share my body and blood? Will you embrace life, friends, and enemies in memory of me? Will you live life, knowing that there will always be enough when you feed, when you serve one another?"

What is the effect on our political and religious creeds and behaviors when we look into the mirror of the paschal meal? Do we represent, re-present, the body and blood of Jesus? Do we do this, not only at our church tables, but beyond our altars and into the lives of the global communion? The mirror of this Last Supper re-flects Jesus asking us: "Will you be my body?

Will you be my blood? Will you remember me?" *Mira!*

A Mirror For Observing The Cross
We have many devotional rituals that help us to re-flect with the story of Good Friday. Each is a facet of this paschal mystery. There are the psalms of suffering, the gospel stories, movies, symphonies, passion plays, and operas like "Godspell" and "Jesus Christ Super-star." In this mirror, I share a story with you. It is one that was revealed through a ceremony of a woman's public profession of vows as a sister of a religious order. It is a story about the effect one person can have on another's life. It is a story that reveals a question that the cross re-flects to all of us. *Mira!*

●●●

Meg told me that she had re-flected many times on the values that her younger sister had effected within her family. This sister was differently abled in body and mind. And she certainly was specially abled! She had been "sabbath bread" for the entire family. Her differences had enabled all of them to embrace many difficult and joyous experiences with new eyes.

Now, at this celebrative time of Meg's life commit-ment, she wanted her enabling sister to be a witnessing minister during the ceremony. However, she was hav-ing a problem because so much of the "church" ritual was not empowering of any women, not even she who was making the commitment, let alone a differently abled woman. As she searched she remembered the processional cross. Her sister could carry this symbol in the entrance and recessional processions.

When the family members arrived at the church for the ceremony, the professing woman practiced the pro-cession rituals with her sister. Meg wanted it all to be perfect, so she said to her sister, "Let's go through this again." With the cross in front of her face, the different-ly abled sister looked at Meg and said, "I know what I am doing! Do you know what you are doing with your life?"

●●●

Every time I look at a cross, I hear those word read-dressed to me: "I know what I am doing! Do you know what you are doing with your life?" I keep looking and I see more! Look with me. *Mira!*

We see a dying human being who hangs, during the final breaths of his life, with non-grasping hands. We see a man who with hands and feet nailed to the wood still embraces a mother and a friend with care, who touches persecutors with reconciliation, and who hands over life with faithfulness. We encounter a human being who refuses to clutch at status, fame, power or relationships, but who continues to breathe in relation-ship with the source of life. Could it be that the way he remained sinless was that he never grasped at life, even until this death on a cross? Perhaps that is what freedom looks like: To breathe with all the life one has, and finally to breathe one's last breath into the source, the first giver of breath itself.

In the mirror of Good Friday, the namer of the in-discriminately gracious sacred teaches us the meaning of salvation: "Embrace life. In the embrace you will ex-perience joy and pain, pleasure and sadness, life and death. But do not grasp. Grasping makes false idols of that which you clutch to yourself. Instead, with open, worshipping hands, be ready for more life. Cherish life. Relish it. Every embrace issues the freedom of choice to let go for more. Such is the way of the Kin-dom."

The cross is a sign of Jesus the Christ who spent his life embracing the Sacred/Creating/Relating mystery. Such is its message. Such is its blessing. The cross is a sign of a way of life that is totally involved with all of life. It challenges us to mutuality and involvement with life. It is not a sign of domination. The cross condemns any form of dominating relationship.

The re-flection of Good Friday is Jesus' redeeming

power being issued to all of humankind: "Trust Life.
Watch your life for the revelation of the Kin-dom. Then
embrace it with faithful gratitude until the end. Salvation is yours. *Mira!*"

A Mirror For Observing The Resurrection

For all who were involved with Jesus, the resurrection was more than they had ever expected! And that
new life of the Christ continues to be the most intan-
gible mystery of our faith. Yet, because of the resurrection, all of our lives' tangible responses are filled with
more power than we could ever attain by our own
grace. And our faith re-flects the promise of even more
life! Resurrection! *Mira!*

When we Christians commemorate this mystery,
we ritualize the "changed yet real" human life of Jesus
Christ with vibrant celebrations. We bless new light,
new water, and new life. We wear new clothes and
breakout of old shells and holes. We sing our "Al-
leluias" with renewed energy because we believe that
death has lost its grasping hold on us. Jesus is resurrected! We re-flect this to all the earth on Easter Sunday.

What do the events of the Easter morning mirror for
our lives today? What questions do they pose? *Mira!*

We see a rock moved by a power beyond ordinary
expectation. We see an unexplainable light that an-
nounces changed life. What are the rocks of our lives
that need to be moved so that more life can breathe
freely? Do we find ourselves clinging to the rock because we are afraid of new, changed, or different life
experiences? Do we allow this mysterious power to
challenge us, to unblock the tombs of our fears, and to
let the life within the tomb be transformed?

In this mirror we also see a garden where a
woman's tears clear her eyes to see whom she desires,
Jesus the namer. "Mary," he says, calling the Mag-
dalene by name. And the woman who once was brought
before Jesus in order that he would name her to death,

is now named whole by the Christ of all life. She is commissioned to be the first namer of this newly revealed power. It is Mary who names the truth of the resurrection to others.

Being called by name can release all of us from sadness, losses, tears, and the desires to clutch life. Being called by name can empower us to be the revealer of truth to others. Like Mary, we are each commissioned by name to share the good news: life is more than expected—resurrection. We need to cry out our desire, listen for our name, and dare to tell the kin. The good news will issue reconciliation—Kin-dom harmony in its fullest revelation.

The mirror of the resurrection re-flects that Christ appeared wherever people were gathered: in upper rooms, at lakeside shores, on roads between towns, at the end of fishing trips, and during the sharing of meals and stories. It alerts us to be awake and ready for such encounters with more than expected life. *Mira!*

Questions and Suggestions for Re-flection

● What effect have the paschal events had on your life up until your reading of this re-flection?

● How do you experience and describe the mystery of a meal?

● How do you experience and describe sin?

● How do you experience and describe resurrection?

● Do you relate with others from a dominating stance or from a mutual, relating vision?

● What is the message of the cross for you?

● Scan the gospels and take note of:
    all the meals that Jesus shares.
    all the meal images that Jesus preaches.
    all the temptations to grasp at life that he ex-
    periences.
    all the healing embraces that he extends to others.

● Record your responses to the questions within this
Re-flection.

● When are you tempted to grasp life?

● When are you most free to embrace life?

● How does your community celebrate the paschal
events?

RE-FLECTION 10

Becoming Church

"My God and my all!" This is the prayer, the radical life response, that Francis of Assisi exclaimed as he lived in relationship to his God's call, "Go, rebuild my church." This was his creed. He believed and professed that the Kin-dom was revealed everywhere. At the end of his life, Francis was physically blind. But he continued to see the presence of the Kin-dom because of the power of the sacred that had webbed its mystery within his life. Thus his final blessing and exhortation to his companions was: "I have done my part; may Christ teach you yours."

Francis arrived at this moment of fullness through a lifetime struggle of sacred-searching. As we journey our course into intimacy with the sacred we have his story to challenge and encourage us. He re-flects a life that makes possible the rebuilding of church by representing Christ with all of creation.

When Francis died, his companions desired to make his absence present. This is the sentiment of all discipleship in the wake of the loss of an inspirational guide and companion. This was the sentiment of the disciples of Jesus. He had left a blessing and an exhortation to them that Francis' only imitated. The Christ commissioned the disciples: "Full authority has been given to me in heaven and on earth. Go, therefore, and make disciples of all nations." (Mt. 28:16)

We can see that both Jesus' and Francis' departing mission statements were about beginnings. They were

words that emowered transition and transformation.
The kin who received the blessings immediately felt the
absence of the enabler. From the depths of that experience of "absence desiring presence," they cried out
for continuing life. Within Jesus' disciples, the power of
"absence desiring presence" burned away their fears
until they were so inflamed that they burst forth, like
from the womb, from the upper room proclaiming and
witnessing the spirit's presence. We name this transformation "pentecost." It is the re-flection among the
kin of the midwifing spirit of Christ's power and love. It
is the becoming of church.

What does church look like? Consider the cobweb.
The facets and touching particles of it all contribute to
its reality; however, without the whole webbing we
would not see the facets or particles. The same is true of
all mysteries as they are in the process of becoming
known and experienced realities. The following facets
highlight a few of the revelations of the mystery we
name "church." There are others for you to discover.
Together, with the midwifing spirit, you are becoming
the mission and message of Jesus Christ: the becoming
church. *Mira!*

A Facet

When I was in third grade, I learned to spell the
word "church." I thought that I already knew most of
what "church" was about, for by the age of nine I was
familiar with its buildings and gatherings. I knew about
family prayer, community prayer, and quite a few other
devotions. I knew priests and sisters and I was experienced in processions and collections. I had already
spent significant times in rectories, convents, and even
in a seminary. However, I was about to see a new vision, a truth about church that would deeply affect my
life.

The teacher said that the word "church" was easy
to spell. First, we were told that the outside structures of
the word were both the same: "ch." All we had to re-

member was what was in the center. YOU ARE what makes the word a living reality. Within the structures, "UR" the life of the church.

Third grade is a faraway memory. I have a hazy recollection of the boy that I "fell in love with" that year. I think I thought that I was well on my way in life. Don't all nine year olds? But this learning that I, rather that we, are the church was revolutionary. Conversion began. It has, over the years, drawn me into personal involvement with others. It has lured me into many participatory movements. It has challenged my selfishness and encouraged me to be a conspirator—to breath with the spirit. I often give thanks for my third grade teacher's wisdom. That spelling lesson was one of the most formational ecclesiology courses that I have ever experienced.

A Facet:

"These remained faithful to the teachings. All lived in common; they sold their goods and possessions and shared the proceeds among themselves according to what each one needed. They went as a body to the temple everyday but met in their homes for the breaking of the bread; they shared their food gladly and generously; they praised God and were looked up to by others." (Acts 2:42-47)

A Facet:

The church has tried to describe herself through different images. Images effect and re-flect our behaviors. Here are some of the images that history reveals:

The body of Christ
The people of God
The life of the Spirit
The bride of Christ
Holy Mother
Fellowship

Ark of the Covenant
The bark of Peter
A communion with the apostles

A Facet:
Webster's Dictionary (1984) lists seven definitions
for the noun "church":
1. The company of all Christians considered
as a mystic, spiritual body.
2. A building for public, especially Christian, worship.
3. A congregation.
4. Public divine worship in a church.
5. A specified Christian denomination.
6. Ecclesiastical power.
7. The clerical profession.

A Facet:
In his book, *Models of the Church* (1974), Avery
Dulles, S.J., delineates the following five models of the
church: Institution, Community, Sacrament, Herald,
and Servant. To briefly explain, church as Institution is
a church of ministers (hierarchy) who are responsible
to the laity for teaching, sanctifying, and ruling. Church
as Community is a people united interiorly in belief,
worship, and companionship in order to lead others into
communion with God. Church as Sacrament envisions
itself as a worshiping community of believers who by
their faith become a sign and instrument of the union of
God and humankind. Church as Herald is present when
a faithful people hear the word of God, treasure it, and
proclaim the Jesus event through their lives. And
church is Servant when it acts as a redeemed people
who have the mandate to establish, in the world, the
kin-dom of peace, justice, love, and reconciliation.
Each of these models has its strengths, weaknesses,
and tensions. Rarely do they stand nakedly alone. Their
combining facets reveal the mystery. And it is always
changing. This constant becoming is what Dulles
describes in another book as "the resilient church."

A Facet:

Once there was a renowned tightrope walker in a traveling circus. Whenever the circus came to town, the people would gather with great enthusiasm to experience Bernie's feats. They would watch, hold their breath, cry, and scream. Applauds were constant. Everyone was fascinated. And they always wanted more of Bernie's act.

One afternoon the ringmaster announced, "Ladies and gentlemen, boys and girls! Bernie is here!" As the welcome thundered, Bernie tumbled into the ring and climbed up to the platform at one end of the netless tightrope. Then silence filled the tent as she cautiously made her way across the rope. This tension exploded with applause when she reached the other end.

Bernie continued to play with the crowd's fascination and terror as she went back and forth across the rope, high above the ring. First, she dazzled them by doing it while blindfolded! Then she rode a unicycle while holding a balancing rod! Finally, she rode the unicycle while she was blindfolded! When she lowered herself down to the ring level the crowd roared with approval and ecstasy: "More! More!" they chanted. "More!"

Bernie held her hands up and quieted the crowd. Then she described her encore.

"I will ride the unicycle across the rope, but this time I will not use the balancing rod. Instead, I will pull this one-wheeled cart behind me. Do you want me to try it?"

"Yes! Yes! Yes!" The crowd pleaded, "Bernie! Bernie!"

"I must be extremely alert when I do this," she warned them, "So, please, may I have your silence!?"

In the hush of the anxious, fascinated observers, Bernie climbed again to the platform, taking her one—wheeled cart with her. Then, high above the ring, she began her amazing act. She was only two cycle revolutions onto the rope when she reversed her direction. When she got back to the platform she stood and looked intensely at the silent crowd. All eyes were focused upon her, so everyone saw her point her finger at one of the onlookers. Then, as they moved their gaze toward that person, they heard Bernie's invitation.

"You, there. Yes. You! Will you come up here with me and get into this cart as I do my act? Will you participate in the daring?"

Ladies and gentlemen! Brothers and sisters! Each "becoming church act" is a possible re-flection of the Kin-dom of God. Will you get into the cart? Will you participate in the daring? As you consider your response, remember the words that Jesus invited us to pray: "May thy Kin-dom come, on earth, as it is in heaven."

Questions and Suggestions for Re-flection

● Getting involved with exploring a mystery takes time. It is work. No one can do the work for us. Each of us must participate in the process and in the tensions. Take sabbath space and time to re-flect and record your work with these questions as they relate to the previous facets.

● When did the mystery of church begin to come alive in your life? What effects has that had on your relationship to church throughout the years?

● How does your experience of church today re-flect the early church experience as recorded in Acts? How does your church make the absent Jesus present?

● As a people, are we a gracious revelation of the Kin-dom?

● How would you describe church? How do you think that observers would describe your church? What does your church's behavior re-flect?

● What would you add to or eliminate from Webster's definitions of church? How would you define church as a verb?

● When have you received and/or shared in church as:

Institution?
Community?
Sacrament?
Herald?
Servant?
Resilient?
_____?

● Do you read and re-flect with the studies and teachings, the policies and values of your church?

● Do you consider yourself a fully participating member?

● How are you and your communion becoming church?

RE-FLECTION 11

*Conversion
Into Originality*

Conversion and conversation are each rooted in the process of "turning with." To live in such revolution with all of creation while grasping at nothing (no thing) is the virgin core of the Christian lifestyle. Through this way of life, we learn to re-flect our originality. We come to know our truth, our life source as God first knew us: "Oh, you are so good!" (Genesis 1:31)

What does conversion into originality look like? First, we must recognize that we only glimpse particles or facets of it. Second, a way of life is a dynamic process. It is always turning with the breath of now. Therefore, even what we see and name is part of the conversion and is itself empowering the person to become more virginally original. Remember that "virgin" means that inner core where we know and are known as creatures of the creating sacred. We can claim the grace of this space.

We can look at some stories. Each of these was related to me during a faith-sharing conversation about what the sacred was webbing in the individuals' lives. Each person was committed to re-flective space and sabbath time. *Mira!*

●●●

Bob is an adult Christian, son, husband, father and professional. Through many years of re-flection and

spiritual exercises, in and through his ordinary commitments and relationships to life, he became aware of a
darkness that was grasping at his spirit. It was in the
mirror of this darkness that he first saw its form. Somehow it was all connected to the message his mother had
communicated about his birth. She had wanted a
female child. He was a disappointment. Once Bob recognized his memory of this message it opened him to
vistas of past and present behaviors and compulsions.
He realized that he had swallowed his mother's senti-
ments as a truth about himself: He was a disappointment! He had generalized this to all that he did and to
all of his relationships. This was the darkness that
needed to be released. He needed a conversion into his
original created goodness. He had to stop judging himself in comparison to a non-truth that he had ingested.

Bob began the work of desiring conversion. He entered into conversations with kin who could companion
the revolution of his imagination and behaviors. In the
midst of the process, the family hosted his mother for a
week-long visit. When she arrived she presented Bob
with some ham because she said that it was his favorite
food. The ham sat in the refrigerator during the week
because it really wasn't Bob's favorite food.

The evening before his mother was to leave, Bob
and his wife were in conversation about the next morning's brunch. They wanted it to be special. They
decided to use the ham because his mother would like
that. Bob got it from the refrigerator to see
if it was still fresh. He took a bite. It was rancid. He spit
it out. That was the moment of recognition for him. He
had not swallowed a message from his mother. He
would dare to disappoint her by saying that the ham had
spoiled. He would name that truth and not blame himself for letting the ham spoil.

In conversation with his mother about the ham, Bob
also named the other memories and insights he was
turning with in relationship to her. Of course these
were not her memories. It really didn't matter. Bob did

not have the need to blame her. He had the need for conversion, for healing, for reconciliation of his memories. In spitting out the ham, Bob had embraced a grace that would lure him to his original goodness. Commitment to a re-flective way of life was empowering Bob in his conversion toward the way of the Kin-dom.

Diane was participating in her fifth experience of Sabbath Space. One of her constant cries was for more time in her life in order to re-flect, to read, to participate in the natural ecstasies of life, and to feel more relaxed rather than rushed. She found herself always naming this desire while in the midst and messes of her commitments to family, profession, and church. Why then, she asked herself, was she making this new commitment to another time-consuming process?

Through conversations with the companions of Sabbath Space, Diane came to recognize that the desire she uttered needed to be practiced in behavior. Sabbath Space was like a yearly mecca for her. Through its discipline she could see her desire more clearly. In its mirror she could imagine the possibilities that she needed to embrace so that her life would convert into more harmony—Kin-dom harmony.

John is an interior decorator. He is proud of his work. He envisions it as a way to make holy the home-spaces he beautifies. He usually works alone and he loves the solitude. This ministerial attitude is affirmed by his many satisfied customers. He is always on the way to another job.

On one particular afternoon, John was stopping by a new customer's home to see what she had called him to estimate. When he pulled his van into the driveway, he heard a woman call out to him from inside. She inquired if it was he and then told him to let himself in the back door. She was sitting at the kitchen counter.

Loraine introduced herself and offered John some coffee and cookies. Then she went into a long discourse about why she needed some ceilings and walls redone. John listened but was mostly aware of his compulsion for her to get on with it. He wanted to see the rooms and do the estimate so that he could be on his way to another job. His time was precious to him. But she seemed to be in no hurry. She talked on and on. Finally, she asked him if he wanted to see the rooms. Trying not to sound as agitated as he felt, he told her that that would be a good idea.

Loraine braced her body with her arms on the kitchen counter. Slowly, she let herself down to the floor. Then, laying on her stomach, she pulled herself with her arms toward the front rooms. John was still in shock when she turned her head around and playfully told him not to step on her. Her humor in the midst of his horror re-flected on his compulsions like lightning.

When they reached the room where one of the ceilings needed redecorating, Loraine laid on her stomach, with her head in her hands, and continued to talk to John. He, however, felt a new compulsion, a compulsion in the process of conversion. He laid down on the floor and did the rest of his work with his hands holding up his head. At that level, eye to eye, he knew the mutuality and compassion of his God. Through that conversation John was able to name and proclaim some of his originality as kin of the earth. And he saw, in the mirror of a differently abled woman, the behavior that was necessary in order to image the Kin-dom of God.

●●●

Originality is the virgin core of every human being's beginning and end. It is our primal grace. It is the power we breathe as we choose to live in contemplative intimacy with the sacred. It has been so since the dawn of creation, for so it was that "In the beginning was God." And that pregnant spirit issued life. From the waters of the sacred, there gushed forth all goodness, all resources, and all relationships. The God of graciousness, compassion, and harmony breathed creation into being out of her sacred imagination of abundant and complete possibility. Our virgin imaginations know this. It is the equality and diversity, the freedom and shared power, the harmony and mutuality for which we each yearn, strain, and search.

However, we also remember the rest of the story. Somewhere, somehow, someone was not satisfied and grasped at a bit of the abundance. It was only a small part that was clutched, but the act was all that was needed to break the fragile webbing of original creation. Perhaps it was as small a particle as the desire for "mine" rather than the celebration of "ours." Whatever and whomever it was, we know, through remembered and experienced life, that we now deal with the disharmony. Yet, within the chaos of such separation from originality, we still repeatedly breathe our desires for the ways of the virgin beginning.

One of the challenges to all of us who yearn for originally created harmony is to seek reconciliation by again entering into conversation with the cosmos. We need to bond together and search for ways to turn with the rest of creation. Domination, compulsion, comparison, and competition must be abandoned if we are to ever be at home within the Kin-dom that issued creation.

Where do we begin? Which of our broken visions of daily experience do we focus upon first? What needs conversion? What doesn't need conversion! *Mira!* Conversion is a call that requires the response of conscience and consciousness. Conversion cannot be legislated. The choice is ours.

Many of us kin of today's global experience find ourselves imprisoned by our own attitudes and behaviors of comparison. This is evidenced in our opinions, cultural practices, economic controls, race relationships, status-focused rituals and worshipping services, educational methods, and gender prejudices.

We are afraid of the power of our virgin selves. Comparison living is not true to original creation. We need conversion into a kin who gratefully accept life with all of its differently enabling gifts. Will we choose to allow the spirit to convert us into re-flections of the indiscriminately gracious sacred? Can we learn to name and claim our originality rather than compare our differences unto the death of all of us?

Another death-dealing way that needs conversion is our competitive way of relating. We set ourselves up as a norm and then expect others to match up. Or, we let a sinful, grasping institution legislate the standard, and we blindly work towards beating the mark. Neither behavior images original power or grace. Originality is smothered by our envy, lechery and put-downs. Can we choose, instead, a way of re-flecting life, a spirituality, that will re-create us, that will reconcile us as a people of compassion? Will we choose mutuality rather that competitions?

Yet, another vision of broken harmony is our compulsive behaviors and lifestyles. We want to control all power and everyone's use of grace. We especially want to control our own time, space, and relationships. Therefore, we grasp at powers that we think we can use to remake the cosmos in our image and likeness. "More is better!" is the value that runs our governments' policies, our food supplies, our use of the earth's resources, our ammunition depots, and our compulsive dealings with ourselves and others. The hell of such compulsive behaviors is the fear and the anxiety that destroys all freedom. We lose our power to remember original goodness and its gracious ways. Will we respond to the prophets, the poor among the kin, who call us to conversion? Will we embrace a way of life that reflects the beatitude of all creation? Will we enter conversations that hold the possibility for freedom? Will we let go of our compulsions for the sake of Kin-dom harmony?

Envisioning originality means an abandonment of

dualistic thinking, imaging, and behaving. This is not an easy conversion. For at least the last four millennium, humankind has lived under the death-dealing ways of patriarchy, the protector of dualism. Almost all of us kin of the earth have forgotten the original ways of relating. We need a healing of our memories, our behaviors, and our ways of organizing and communing. We need to turn with the originality of created goodness. We need to choose to re-flect the ways of our indiscriminately gracious creator.

How? One possibility is to enter into conversation with each other about our images of the sacred. And in the midst of these conversions we need to watch our language. When we use exclusive images, whether when referring to the sacred or to the kin, we need to choose to convert those images into inclusive words and symbols. This conversion process cannot happen if we live in isolation from one another's differing gifts. We need each other to "turn with" our original, virginally created goodness. We need each other, all the kin of the earth, to fully re-flect the Kin-dom of God.

Other possibilities of conversion toward originality might be to begin to affirm each other's specialness rather than to compare and compete with each other's faults and/or virtues. We can also begin to claim our original blessings rather than grasp at our original sins. We can forgive ourselves and each other our mistakes and failings. We can laugh more. We can throw more parties instead of wars. We can choose to live responsibly as our sisters' and brothers' keepers. We can remember to quote our God more often as we behold originality in any of its revelations: "Oh, you are so good!"

Questions and Suggestions for Re-flection

● When you hear the word "original," what do you image? Do you image grace? Do you image sin?

● Can you remember and name a conversion experience of your life?

● What comparative, competitive, and/or compulsive images, values, or behaviors need conversion in your life? How will you enter the process? With whom? Why?

● Is your language inclusive of all of creation's possibilities?

● Is the language of your community's prayer, rituals, or behaviors in need of conversion?

● How do the conversations that you participate in midwife conversion and discipleship?

● When are you most originally yourself? Do you name that as a grace?

● When, where, and with whom do you proclaim: "You are so good!"?

III.
SAMPLE
COMMUNITY
SABBATHS

HOW TO RE-FLECT
AS A COMMUNITY

Sabbath Bread is an invitation to conversion. The process is continuous and challenging. The Mirrors and the Re-flections of this book have provided some ways to search and re-flect with the mysteries of our faith. The question remains: "How do we share the wisdom that the spirit webs? How do we come to be a community of faith-sharing folk who affect the spirituality of one another for the sake of the Kin-dom?"

First, I believe, we must root ourselves in the grounding truth that we are our sisters' and brothers' keepers. We must accept the responsibilities of our stewardship of the earth and all of creation. Our creed must be proclaimed through our lives of relationship and virgin prayer. A prophet of the earth has said it for us:

> This we know. All things are connected like the blood which unites one family. Whatever befalls the earth befalls the children of the earth. We did not weave the web of life, we are merely a strain in it. Whatever we do to the web, we do to ourselves.
> —Adapted from an oration by Chief Seattle, 1854

In this ground the desire to gather, to commune, to share our faith will take root and grow to fruitfulness. Even though this section of *Sabbath Bread* offers some suggestions on how a faith-sharing community can use the Mirrors and the Re-flections of the book, it is important to recognize that not every community begins with such processes. Here is a story of how one group became a faith-sharing community. It is a story of a "bridge group."

A group of women gathered once a month to play cards. For years they relaxed this way. Then at one of the gatherings, one of the women raised a question. Something was bothering her about a local political issue. It didn't fit with her values. There were a few nods among the other women and a few remarks were offered. But after a short while, someone reminded them that they had come together to play bridge.

At the next month's bridge club gathering, another woman said that she'd been gnawed by the previous month's question. She began offering her thoughts as someone else dealt the first hand of cards. Then there was a pause while conversation revolved around the issue. Finally, the reminder to play cards was sounded.

Over the next several months, the conversations embraced more and more of the time. At one of the gatherings, when the reminder, "We are a bridge group! Let's play cards!" was spoken, one of the women said, "Look. Let's process what has been happening over this period of our gathering." Through the conversation that followed, they came to see that they were still meeting in the name of playing cards, but lately they were rarely playing cards. Instead they were resourcing each other in their search for meaning and direction in their lives.

A common re-flection and the naming of the process led these women to a new choice. Today they still gather. They even continue to call themselves "The Bridge Group." But now they no longer take the cards out of the box. Instead they bring their lives to this sacred-searching and faith-sharing monthly gathering of friends.

This section of *Sabbath Bread* presents three differently timed possibilities for processing the Reflections. One is an eleven-session experience called Sabbath Space. This process can be used as a guide in a communal setting over an eleven-week or an eleven-

month timespan. The second is a design for processing
the book's re-flections on the mysteries of the Christian
faith over a seven-session experience. The third process
is a way of using Sabbath Bread during a weekend or
three-day gathering of folk. All of these repeatable
group processes are designed with the hope that the
leader or group facilitator, the hosting companion of a
faith-sharing community, will use them as a guide. They
are suggestions that the author has used over the past
several years. Yet they are only seeds for your planting.
Be creative. Web the wisdom of Sabbath Bread with the
needs and hopes of your communion. Mira!

COMMUNITY SABBATH 1

Sabbath Space in Eleven Sessions

Setting the scene:
These sessions are designed for a suggested 2 to 2½-hour sabbath gathering space. It is recommended that there not be more than ten community participants. If the community is larger, gather as two or more sharing groups. Each session has the following four dynamics: Gathering Prayer, Sharing Space, Re-flecting Space, and Missioning Prayer. The first two dynamics can be experienced as a unit, and the second two as another unit with a break for refreshment between them. Often the first two dynamics take more than half of the gathering time. That is one reason why it is important that each participant have a personal copy of *Sabbath Bread*. In that way they can use their personal sabbath space between gatherings to re-flect on the focused mystery of the session.

The Gathering Prayer is a communal expression of praise and thanksgiving, of silence and expressed words or rituals. Two prayers that appear in the Reflections are often used by the community during this time. This dynamic helps all of the participants to become present to the "now" of Sabbath Space.

Each companion is a participant. Each companion, including the hosting companion or facilitator, is expected to share during the Sharing Space. Thus, this dynamic begins within an environment of silence dur-

ing which the participants review their journals or recorded memories of how the sacred has been webbing
mystery in and through their ordinary, daily, lived experience. They review this graced movement in their
lives since the last gathering time.

After a significant time of silence for the purpose of
recall and for making a choice of what to appropriately
share with the community, the hosting companion invites each person around the circle to share their re-
flected wisdom. All the other companions listen with attention. If it seems appropriate, some affirmation or
gentle questioning can be offered to the one who is
sharing. However, it is very inappropriate to comment
in any form that tells one how she or he ought to feel or
deal with whatever is being shared. This makes a problem out of the mystery that is being looked at. Sabbath
Space is for faith-sharing. It is not for problem solving.

Confidentiality is also a reverenced gift that each
companion offers to each other through Sabbath Space.
Even when good friends, couples or members of the
same family or community participate in Sabbath
Space, it is important that what is expressed during the
Sharing Space is not talked about outside of that space.
If a companion wishes to converse with another companion about her or his sharing, one is to ask if that
would be the desire of the other. Sometimes what we
express in faith community is new, even to us, and we
need time to re-flect with it before we continue to speak
about it. And sometimes we just do not want to process
it beyond the grace of the mystery. The choice to continue conversation about what was shared is always the
choice of the companion who named the experience.

After all of the companions have shared their wisdom webbings, the community gathers for re-flection
and conversation about another faith mystery. Thus,
another Re-flection is processed. The facilitator or hosting companion is the usual presenter of this Re-flecting
Space, but the process can be delegated to another companion. The conversations that revolve around the

newly focused mystery are for the purpose of conversion. They are invitations to *mira*. They are challenges to look at a mystery from a different facet of the webbings than how we may be used to seeing life. Again, "shoulds" or "oughts" are to be avoided.

After this dynamic the community is commissioned to continue to process the mystery through their individual sabbath space experience until the next gathering. During this Missioning Prayer dynamic, they are reminded of their covenant commitment to take space, at least 15 minutes a day, for significant individual sabbaths. Some folk may take an hour twice a week. However one chooses, individual sabbath space is necessary in order to review the focused Re-flection, to re-flect with the questions and suggestions that follow each Re-flection, and to record the graces of their sabbaths with their unique journaling style. Then, in and with prayer, all of the community blesses each other for this mission.

These are the dynamics of Sabbath Space. Sabbath blessings of wisdom! *Mira!*

SABBATH SPACE 1

Gathering Prayer:
  The hosting companion invites the community to re-
flection with music of her or his choice. Then the prayer
at the end of Re-flection 3 is prayed with the group.

Sharing Space:
  Each companion introduces herself or himself in
three ways:
  ● first, by their full and preferred name.
  ● second, by a playful name someone may
    have given to them. The story of this can be told.
  ● third, by a spiritual name or image they have or
    a wisdom that they desire.

Re-flecting Space:
  The hosting companion presents the contents of the
Explanation, The Mirrors, and Re-flection 1 of *Sabbath
Bread*. She or he has prepared this prior to the first
gathering. Because this is the initial session, the input of
content and setting the scene takes the majority of the
time of this session.
  The companions converse about their covenant
with each other and share any questions that they may
have about the expectation or process of Sabbath
Space.

Missioning Prayer
  The community members are missioned by the
hosting companion to process these facets during the
time between this and the next session. Each companion is to do the following:

1. Read the Explanation, The Mirrors, and Re-flection 1 of *Sabbath Bread.*
2. Explore and choose a space in their daily or weekly routine for sabbath.
3. Explore and choose a journaling style and establish a routine for recording or collecting the memories of each individual sabbath.
4. During some individual sabbath spaces, process either the exercise of Mirror 9 or some of the questions and suggestions that follow Re-flection 1.

All pray for daily bread with the prayer found in Re-flection 1.

SABBATH SPACE 2

Gathering Prayer:
    The hosting companion passes a mirror
among the community and invites each one to
take a time and space to *mira*. Soft music can be
played in the background during this experience. When all have had the time to *mira*,
the host/hostess proclaims the prayer that concludes Re-flection 3.

Sharing Space:
    Individually and silently, each companion
reviews their journaling processes since the first
session. After this each one shares how they
lived their covenant since the last gathering.

Re-flecting Space:
    Together, the companions read Mirror 10.
Then one tells the story, as she or he recalls it, of
a Jesus parable. After the telling, the community
discusses the following questions in relationship
to this parable: What was Jesus saying to the
original hearers of this parable? What is the
parable imaging about the Kin-dom of God?
What does this parable re-flect to us about our
daily, lived experience?
    This process of telling a parable and re-
flecting with the three questions is repeated
once or twice, as time permits.
    Re-flection 2 is read and the same three
questions are used as a mirror for *mira*.

Missioning Prayer:
The hosting companion missions the community to do the following:

1. Continue the above process with other parables and record some of their insights with their journaling style.
2. Pray with the questions and suggestions that follow Re-flection 2 during their sabbath spaces.

The community breaks bread with each other as a blessing. The ritual is concluded with the prayer found in Re-flection 1.

SABBATH SPACE 3

Gathering Prayer:
   The hosting companion gathers the community by rereading the parable of Re-flection 2. Music can companion this reading.

Sharing Space:
   Each companion reviews their journaling processes since the previous gathering. Then each shares how the parables critique and affirm their everyday lives.

Re-flecting Space:
   The hosting companion leads the gathered community in exploring the images of Re-flection 3. The community converses about the connections and webbings that each "watching" image elicits form themselves.
   Mirror 9 is presented.

Missioning Prayer:
   The hosting companion missions the community to:
   1. Experience the process described in Mirror 11. The individual chooses her or his own time to live through this process.
   2. Pray with the questions and suggestions that follow Re-flection 3.
   3. Continue to use their journaling style to collect the wisdom of their individual sabbaths.

   All are invited to pray the words that conclude Reflection 3.

SABBATH SPACE 4

Gathering Prayer:
   The hosting companion leads the group in
prayer with the prayer that concludes Re-flection 3.

Sharing Space:
   The community reviews their sabbath journaling processes. Then the individuals share the images that were re-flected to them as they have been
watching their life since the last gathering.

Re-flecting Space:
   The hosting companion invites each member to recall a significant community experience of their life.
They are invited to share their memory in relationship
to these questions: What happened? How did that experience invite or challenge me to Christian discipleship? How did that experience inspire me to live my
Christian values?
   The facilitator can use Re-flection 4 to help guide
this conversation.

Missioning Prayer:
   Each companion is missioned to do the following:

   1. Read and re-flect with Re-flection 4 and
      the questions and suggestions that follow it.
   2. Process the exercise of Mirror 12.

The companions form a circle and hold hands. Each names a need that they would like the community to hold in their hearts during the week. By doing so each companion midwifes life to greater fullness in the others. Then the hosting companion puts some salt in each person's hand. In silence, each is asked to ex-perience the salt and to re-flect on why it is that Jesus said, "You are the salt of the earth." Then each shares their wisdom. When this sharing is concluded, each person puts their salt on a common dish with the words: "We are the salt of the earth." The community observes that they can no longer take back their individual salt. A sign of peace is shared with the words: "You are the salt of the earth."

SABBATH SPACE 5

Gathering Prayer:
   The hosting companion invites the community to bless and break bread with each other as a sign of their covenant. The ritual is concluded with the prayer found in Re-flection 1.

Sharing Space:
   Time is taken to review the journaling process that each companion has recorded with her or his preferred style. Then the facilitator invites each one to share the wisdom of these webbings since the last gathering.

Re-flecting Space:
   The hosting companion presents the basic content of Re-flection 5. When she or he concludes this, the companions are to re-flect on what one or two questions this Re-flection issued in their minds. The questions are all shared. Then discussion can happen in reference to any of the questions.

Missioning Prayer:
   The community is missioned to process the questions and suggestions that follow Re-flection 5 and to record their further questions and wisdom with their journaling style.
   A song or hymn is played or sung as a thanksgiving and blessing. The prayer found at the conclusion of Re-flection 3 is said in unison.

SABBATH SPACE 6

Gathering Prayer:
Using music or song, the hosting companion invites the community to silence. Then each is to name an image of the sacred that re-flects some of the mystery of the divine for themselves. As each companion shares this, the community responds with: "God of life, breathe among us."

Sharing Space:
The companions review their collection of wisdom since the last gathering. This is done in silence. Then each shares the webbings or connections of their sabbaths in relationship to their image of God and their daily lived experiences.

Re-flecting Space:
The facilitator leads the community in processing Mirror 3 in relationship to their image of prayer. Then the hosting companion presents Re-flection 6.

Missioning Prayer:
The hosting companion missions the community to reflect with the questions and suggestions that follow Re-flection 6.
Then the community stands in a circle. One by one, each companion enters the center of the circle. The rest of the community prays the blessing of Wisdom upon him or her. This blessing is found at the conclusion of the Explanation of *Sabbath Bread.*

SABBATH SPACE 7

Gathering Prayer:

The hosting companion gathers the community with his or her original or preferred prayer words and/or ritual.

Sharing Space:

The community members review their journaling processes in silence. Then each companion shares about any wisdom they became aware of during their sabbaths since the last gathering.

Re-flecting Space:

The hosting companion presents the stories and facets of Re-flection 7. Afterwards, the community converses about how it is that the mystery of the incarnation is a call to awareness, involvement, stewardship, and justice.

Missioning Prayer:

The community is missioned to do the following:

1. Read Re-flection 7.
2. To list all the questions that this mystery issues for them.
3. Respond to the questions and suggestions that follow the Re-flection.

The community prays the prayer that concludes Re-flection 3.

SABBATH SPACE 8

Gathering Prayer:
   The hosting companion gathers the community with
music and then with one of the prayers found in the Re-
flections.

Sharing Space:
   The companions review their journals, first in silence and then with a brief sharing. Then the hosting
companion presents the facet of the incarnation as the
divine affirmation of humankind. Whenever we affirm
one another, we continue webbing the mystery of the
incarnation. The community then uses this space to affirm one another for one facet of each one's life.

Re-flecting Space:
   The hosting companion presents the facets of Re-
flection 8. Afterwards the community converses about
their images of the ministry of Jesus. The exercise of
Mirror 3 can facilitate this conversation.

Missioning Prayer:
   The community is missioned to do the following:

1. Read Re-flection 8 and respond to the
   questions and suggestions that conclude it.
2. Process Mirror 3 in relationship to Ministry.

   The hosting companion prays for the community
with the words that Jesus prayed at his last supper.
These are recorded in the Gospel of John, Chapter 15.

SABBATH SPACE 9

Gathering Prayer:
   The hosting companion gathers the community with an invitation to silence. After a re-flective time, the community members are each asked to express their spontaneous prayers.

Sharing Space:
   The community members review their journaling processes in silence. Then each companion shares how it was that they spent their sabbaths and the wisdom webbings of such re-flections.

Re-flecting Space:
   The hosting companion presents the three mirrors of the paschal event as illustrated in Re-flection 9. The community converses about questions that such mirrors re-flect to them.

Missioning Prayer:
   The companions are missioned to journal with their responses to the questions and suggestions that conclude Re-flection 9.
   The hosting companion blesses each companion individually with a symbol of the cross and/or resurrection. They are told to bring this symbol with them to the next gathering.

SABBATH SPACE 10

Gathering Prayer:
    The community gathers with their missioning symbols from the previous Sabbath Space. Re-flecting with the symbols, each companion expresses her or his own prayer.

Sharing Space:
    The companions review their journaling processes in silence. Then each one shares the wisdom of their sabbaths since the last gathering.

Re-flecting Space:
    The hosting companion, using bread dough that has been prepared from the recipe that follows, invites each companion to score the dough with a personal image of church. Each one shares why they are choosing this image. When all have shared, the dough is baked.
    While the bread is baking, the hosting companion presents the facets of Re-flection 10 while the group follows along with *Sabbath Bread*. The community shares their re-flections and hopes for becoming church.

Missioning Prayer:
    The community is missioned to read Re-flection 11 and to respond with their journaling style to the questions and suggestions that conclude it.
    The companions then bless each other with the breaking and sharing of the bread. They give bread to each other with these words: "Holy food for holy people. Take and eat."
    All the companions are missioned to bring an

original food creation to the next gathering.

A Bread Recipe

Mix/Sift together:

> 1 C. whole wheat flour
> 1/2 C. white flour
> 3/4 tsp. baking soda
> 1/8 tsp. salt

Then add:

> 2 tblsp. liquid shortening
> 2 tblsp. honey (optional)
> 1/2 C. water

Knead and shape on a greased cookie sheet.
Bake at 375 degrees for 10-12 minutes.

SABBATH SPACE 11

Gathering Prayer:
   The hosting companion invites the community to re-
flection with music. When they are ready, each companion prays spontaneously.

Sharing Space:
   The community members review their journaling
processes since the last gathering in silence. After such
a period, the facilitator issues the question: "Toward
what originality has this Sabbath Space experience
challenged your conversion?" Some more silence is experienced. Then all share the wisdom webbings of this
experience with each other.

Re-flecting Space:
   A party of original foods is celebrated.

Missioning Prayer:
   The Sabbath Space community and their wisdom is
blessed and missioned with the prayer that concludes
the Explanation of *Sabbath Bread*.
   The community is gently challenged to continue to
gather and to use other processes with the Re-flections.
This experience has been the beginning of a Sabbath
Bread Community for the sake of the Kin-dom. How can
the companions continue to web their Kin-dom wisdom?

COMMUNITY SABBATH 2

Sabbath Space
In Seven Sessions

It is indeed a blessing for a faith-sharing community to have the opportunity to gather for five or seven continuous days. Many experiences can be webbed into such a period of sabbath. For example, the "8-8-8 balance" described in Mirror 11 of *Sabbath Bread* can be practiced and processed throughout the time together. Play and celebration can add color and revelation to the communion. The multi-faceted Kindom of God can be played and prayed. There can be ample space for an individual's sabbath needs to be met and for the community's desires for sharing to be fulfilled. The following plan is one possibility for the webbing of these prayer experiences.

Most of the covenants described at the beginning of Sample Community Sabbaths will need to be processed when the group gathers. Either one or a few facilitators are to be designated for the webbing of the processes from day to day. The exercises suggested in this outline require paper, pencils, and/or crayons, paint, clay, and bread-making ingredients and utensils. Each of these plans is designed for an approximate two-hour period.

Of course other possibilities can be webbed with *Sabbath Bread*. The community can process five or seven of the Community Sabbath 1 outlines. Or the plan can begin with the processes found in Community Sabbath 3 and extend the Community Spaces. Or, one or more of the exercises found in The Mirrors can be the essence of individual space with the community space being designed for the faith-sharing of those processes. The possibilities of wisdom webbing are many. Here is one vision.

The blessings of sabbath bread wisdom! *Mira!*

Day 1

Gathering Prayer:
The community gathers and prays the prayer that concludes Re-flection 3.

Community Space:
The designated facilitator presents Re-flection 3.

Individual Space:
Each companion retreats to their sacred space to process the exercise found in Mirror 11.

Community Sharing:
The companions gather in dyads and share the wisdom of their re-flecting exercises.

Day 2

Gathering Prayer:
The prayer that concludes Re-flection 3 is used in the manner described in Community Sabbath 3, Saturday Afternoon.

Community Space:
The designated facilitator presents Re-flection 5.

Individual Space:
Each companion spends this space processing one of the exercises found in Mirror 3 or Mirror 4.

Community Sharing:
The group gathers in triads and shares the web-bings of the above experience.

Day 3

Gathering Prayer:
The prayer is found at the beginning of Re-flection 1.

Community Space:
The designated facilitator presents Re-flection 6.

Individual Space:
Each companion, alone and in silence, processes some of the questions or suggestions that accompany Re-flection 6.

Community Sharing:
The group gathers in dyads to share the wisdom webbings of their individual sabbaths.

Day 4

Gathering Prayer:
The community gathers. The companions review their journaling process in silence. After a period of time the community members pray spontaneously from the ground of their recordings.

Community Space:
The facilitator presents Re-flection 7.

Individual Space:
The companions retreat to their sacred space to process Mirror 3 or 4.

Community Sharing:
    The community gathers and shares the wisdom of their individual sabbath space re-flections.

Day 5

Gathering Prayer:
    The companions pray for their desires. The ritual is concluded with the prayer found at the beginning of Re-flection 1.

Community Space:
    The facilitator presents Re-flection 8.

Individual Space:
    The companions retreat to their sacred space to process their wisdom webbings of Mirror 2.

Community Sharing:*
    The companions return and choose dyads to share the images that their re-flective space issued.

    *Note: If this is the concluding day of the community's time together for sabbath and sharing, then the above Community Space would be differently processed. For an example see Community Sabbath 3, Sunday Morning: Community Space and Missioning Prayer.

Day 6

Gathering Prayer:
    Same as Day 2.

Community Space:
    The facilitator presents Re-flection 9.

Individual Space:
    The companions retreat to their sacred space and process the questions and suggestions that conclude Re-flection 9.

Community Sharing:
The group gathers, forms triads, and shares the webbings of their individual re-flection space.

Day 7

Gathering Prayer:
See Day 2.

Community Sharing:
The facilitator processes the sharing as it is described in
Community Sabbath 1, Sabbath Space 10: Re-flecting Space.

Missioning Prayer:
See Community Sabbath 3, Sunday Morning: Missioning Prayer.

COMMUNITY SABBATH 3
Sabbath Space In A Weekend Session

Perhaps your community will have the opportunity to gather over a weekend for companionship and faith-sharing. The following outlines will be helpful to you. They integrate a few of the exercises in The Mirrors and some of the Re-flections with the processes outlined in the previous eleven-session Sabbath Space experience. These plans are an example of how you can use other parts of *Sabbath Bread* and create a weekend experience for your community.

A weekend retreat or re-flection space is a relatively intense period of sacred-searching and faith-sharing. To facilitate some harmony within this intensity, it is important that the companions enter a covenant prior to the weekend gathering. The facets of the Mirrors on journaling, Re-flection 1, and the introduction to Community Sabbath 1 need to be read and, if possible, discussed prior to the weekend. Each companion can then come with knowledge of the processes of the weekend, and time will not need to be spent determining the expectations of the community.

Each companion should bring what they need for their journaling style and their copy of *Sabbath Bread*. The community ought to designate one, or five, facilitators for the weekend processes. If these facets are attended to before the group gathers for sabbath, the space will breathe with harmony.

Blessings of *mira* and wisdom on your weekend sabbath.

Friday Evening

Gathering Prayer:
    At a comfortable time, after all of the companions have arrived and settled into the space, the designated facilitator invites the community into a quiet atmosphere for prayer. This is done with music, song, chant, and/or a story.
    Each companion is then asked to name their need and desire for the sabbath space gathering. This is done in a form of petitional prayer. The community responds to each petition with: "God of life, breath among us." The ritual is concluded with all the companions praying the prayer that concludes Re-flection 3.

Community Space:
    See Community Sabbath 1, Sabbath Space 1: Sharing Space for this exercise.

Missioning Prayer:
    The companions are missioned by the facilitator to pray with the questions and suggestions of Re-flection 1 before retiring and in the morning until the next community gathering time.

Saturday Morning

Gathering Prayer:
    The designated facilitator passes a mirror among the companions. In the hallowed silence of the circled community each one takes the time they need to *mira*. When all have done so, the community together proclaims the prayer that concludes Re-flection 3 of *Sabbath Bread*.

Individual Space:
    The designated facilitator missions the companions
to an hour of sacred silence. During this space each
member is to process the exercise found in Mirror 3.
The group might read through the exercise together
before they enter the silence so that any questions can
be answered that pertain to the process.

Community Space:
    When the community regathers, Re-flection 5 is
read together. Then the group shares the webbings of
this reflection with the exercise that they processed
during the individual silent space.

Saturday Afternoon

Gathering Prayer:
    The designated facilitator leads the community in a
re-flection on "graciousness," "compassion," and "harmony." This can be done with a simple word-
association sharing among the group members. One
person says the word "graciousness," and then, going
around the circle, each person webs the word that
comes to their mind in relationship to the proclaimed
word. Then the next word is proclaimed and the process
is repeated. The ritual is concluded with the community
proclaiming the prayer found at the end of Re-flection 3
of *Sabbath Bread.*

Community Space:
    The designated facilitator follows the processes of
Community Sabbath 1, Sabbath Space 6: Re-flecting
Space.

Individual Space:
    The companions take some private space to read
Re-flection 7 and to process, with their journaling style,
some of the questions and suggestions that follow the
Re-flection.

Saturday Evening

Gathering Prayer:
    The designated facilitator blesses the community
with the prayer of John's gospel, Chapter 15.

Community Space:
    The facilitator processes Community Sabbath 1,
Sabbath Space 9: Re-flecting Space.

Missioning Prayer:
    Before retiring and when rising in the morning, the
companions are to process at least one of the questions
or suggestions that conclude Re-flection 9. They are to
record their re-flections with their journaling style.

Sunday Morning

Gathering Prayer:
    The designated facilitator invites the community to
re-flect, in silence, with their journaling process in relationship to Re-flection 9. After a significantly long time
the community members are invited to pray spontaneously from the ground of their wisdom re-flections.

Community Space:
    The facilitator follows the process described in
Community Sabbath 1, Sabbath Space 10: Re-flecting
Space.

Missioning Prayer:
    The companions bless each other with the words:
"Holy food for holy people. Take and eat, this is the
bread of our life."
    When all have shared in the bread of life, the com-
munity forms a circle. In turn, each companion enters
the center of the circle, and the community prays the
blessing of wisdom upon her or him. This blessing can
be found at the conclusion of An Explanation in *Sabbath Bread*.